The Four-Minute Customer

"Getting Jazzed about Your People and Quality Management in Your Call Center"

by

Michael Tamer

The North Star

The Big Dipper

Business Navigation

Only two centuries ago, early explorers (adventurous business executives of those bygone days) were guided primarily with a compass and celestial navigation using reference points like the North Star. Today's busy executive also needs guidance systems with just-in-time business intelligence to navigate through the challenges of locating, recruiting, keeping, and growing profitable customers. The Anton Press provides this navigational system through practical, how-to-do-it books for the modern day business executive.

THE
ANTON
PRESS

ISBN 0-9630464-1-1

Dedication

I want to thank my sweet wife, Ditto, for her amazing encouragement and support. She has truly been wonderful.

Special thanks to Phillip Britt, Diane Miller and Betty Psencik for their assistance with the book. To Jon Anton, Bob Furniss, Yvonne Powell, Katherine Kirkpatrick, Judy Waterman and John Kaiser, who all, at one time or another, bugged me over and over to finish what I had started. Guy, Mit, Dan, Bruce—thank you, brothers, for your support.

Just last names here: Beck, McGill, Feeney, Churchville, Durr, Seguin, Smith, Maloney, Gwilliam, Crockett, Waite, Terrill, Hosage, Carreker, Sundby, Surette, Graff, Schiller, MacPherson, Weller, Salowey, Bazany, Pape, Walker, Macdowell, Vandenberg, Humblias, Lee, Mcdermott, Powers, Anthony, Jackson, Tucker, Garelis, Watson, Byleveld, Hurd, Crandall, Benjamin, Patton, Snyder, McCalmont, Newton, Castranova, Biddinger, Ingelsby, Koons, Coleman, Judson, Wagner, Levitt, Thomas, Johnston, and Loo. From each of the foregoing, I learned a lot or a little. Some of it good, some bad, some both; some in the beginning, some in the end. In each case, whatever I learned proved valuable and applicable to this book.

One more thing, I am really proud of my Dad.

TABLE OF CONTENTS

Foreword..vii

Introduction...ix

Section One: Discovering How We Got Where We Are Today..................1

Chapter 1: The True Nature of Call Centers 3
The Four-Minute Market 3
Sales Versus Service...4
A Balancing Act 5
Knowing the When's and Why's 6
Three Basic Elements...8

Chapter 2: In the Beginning 11
The Advent of Call Centers...11
Two Distinct Purposes...11
The Emergence of Alphabet Soup Technology..................12
Early Efforts to Monitor 13
The New Image of Call Centers..13

Chapter 3: Trends That Have Made History 17
The Four Greatest Changes in Call Centers 17
Interactive Voice Response Unit (IVR) or Voice Response
Unit (VRU)...17
The Universal Agent 20
Desktop Technology...22
Call Center Agent as Professional/Career Choice 25

Chapter 4: Into the Information Age.................................29
A Changing Economy 29
Worldwide Enterprise 30
Connection to the Customer..30
Recognition of Around the Clock Support.........................31
Performance Measurement..31
Employee Relations 31

Section Two: Understanding and Motivating Others 33

   Chapter 5: Hierarchy of Needs 35

      The Life Within Call Centers 35

      Survival Mode...35

      Maslow's Hierarchy of Needs 36

      Michael's Call Center Hierarchy of Needs........................37

   Chapter 6: Rose and Jack 41

      Lessons From a Movie...41

      A Stepping Stone 41

      The "Have To's" and the "Want To's" 42

      Fame or Fun?..43

      Two Companies That Are Doing It Right 44

   Chapter 7: The Call Center Garden...47

      It's the People 47

      Budding Employees...48

   Chapter 8: Roses...51

      rose[1] (r$\bar{o}$z)..51

      The Cream of the Crop...51

      How to Make Your Roses Grow 52

   Chapter 9: Daisies 55

      dai·sy (d$\bar{a}'$ z$\bar{e}$) 55

      Low-Maintenance Flowers...55

      Happens all the time, right? Wrong!..................................56

      The Power of Team Rewards 56

   Chapter 10: Weeds 59

      weed[1] (w$\bar{e}$d) 59

      The Undesirables 59

      Four Types of Weeds 59

      Getting Rid of Weeds 61

Chapter 11: Growing a Better Garden 65

Accept the Bell Curve 65

Section Three: Managing Your Call Center 69

Chapter 12: Elevators 71

Sound Bites 71
Driving Forces 71
Competitive Advantage 72
A Strategy and Purpose 74

Chapter 13: Working to Your Pay Scale 81

Analyze Costs 81
Providing Value to Your Company 81
Reassess Your Roses 82
Create a List 83
Find Temporary Jobs 85
Be the Only Guesser in Your Group 85
Get A Different Perspective 86

Chapter 14: Professional Energy Sucker 89

Seagull Management 89
The Sucking Energy Sound 89
Company Martyrs 92

Chapter 15: Supervisors 95

One Tough Job 95
Four Strategies 96

Chapter 16: Agents 101

A Position of Tremendous Potential 101
The Changing Demands of the Call Center Agent 102
Three Strategies 105

Section Four: Measuring Quality 109

Chapter 17: Quantity Versus Quality 111

Which Is More Important? 111

Chapter 18: A Focus on Quality 117
   The Value of Focusing on Quality 117
   Measuring Quality 118
   Areas of Measurement 119
   Benchmarking 122
Chapter 19: Relationships 125
   How Quality Affects the Call Center 125
   Key Interactions 125
Chapter 20: Call Monitoring..131
   Reviews: A Potential for Conflict 131
   Three Common Complaints About Measurement.........131
   Providing Feedback...136
Chapter 21: Reports 139
   The Purpose of Reports...139
   The Shortcomings of Reports..139
   Interactive Detail Versus Average Data......................140
   Reports With Layers 143
Chapter 22: The Issue of Privacy 147
   Government Involvement...147
   Existing Guidelines...148
   New Areas of Monitoring..150
Chapter 23: The Perfect Call Center...................................153
   A Collection of Greatness...153
   Attributes of the Perfect Call Center 153
   Creating Your Own Perfect Call Center.......................157

Section Five: Technology to Increase Productivity 159
Chapter 24: Deposits and Withdrawals...............................161
   Viewing Transactions as Collisions 161
   A Case Study in Meeting Expectations 162
   Keeping Score of Deposits and Withdrawals................164

Chapter 25: Surveys 167

    The Importance of Customer Feedback 167

    Survey Shortcomings.. 167

    Immediate Response Surveys ,,,,,,,,,,,,,,,,,,,,,,,,,,,,,,,,,,,, 168

Chapter 26: Expectations 171

    First Impressions... 171

    New Technologies, New Expectations............................ 172

Chapter 27: A Killer Application for the Web.............................. 179

    A Look At Web Chat... 179

    Work Support Management... 180

    Requirements for Work Support Management.................... 181

    Benefits of Work Support Management........................... 182

Chapter 28: Skills-Based Routing 185

    A Shift in Thinking.. 185

    Keeping It in Perspective 185

Chapter 29: Taking Stock... 189

    Priorities... 189

    Two Important Rules of Life and Business...................... 192

Appendix.. 199

    Statement by Michael Tamer 199

References 205

Index... 207

Author Biography 209

By

Dr. Jon Anton

Purdue University

Center for Customer-Driven Quality

I have been a "fan" of the author of this book, Michael Tamer, for years. When I first met him, he was the President and CEO of Teknekron Infoswitch Inc., a very successful company dedicated to agent monitoring, and coaching software. His personal energy and charisma caught my interest, and later, his professional drive and vision resulted in my admiration.

Early on, I was fortunate to hear Michael present as a keynote speaker to a large audience at a major call center industry event. Again, I was inspired by his message and his passion for the topic. Michael focused completely on the customer service representatives (CSRs) working the front-line of the call center, and the making of what he called a "Top Rep." As he so eloquently explains, on the shoulders of this army of under-appreciated employees, rests the very reputation of most companies. How do we find them? How do we train them? How do we monitor them? How do we motivate them? How do we reward them?

In fact, it was shortly after this event that I challenged Michael to organize his revolutionary ideas into a book so that professionals worldwide could learn and enjoy from his special message about the importance of CSRs. As is Michael's style, he wholeheartedly accepted this new challenge, knowing full well that he had never written a book, and that it would be an enormous effort to undertake, considering his crowded schedule and many other executive responsibilities.

Two years in the making, "The Four Minute Customer" is a unique and special piece of literary achievement. For one, the message is totally and completely new. For another, the content combines practical, day-to-day advice with step-by-step directions on how to make the most of your front-line CSRs. You will enjoy his many views of the call center, including his analogy of the type of people that work on the front-line, namely weeds (the less desirable CSR), daisies (those are average, but important), and, finally, the roses, yes, the roses (those are the superior CSRs that you can always count on to thoroughly satisfy every caller regardless of the circumstance).

This book is for call center managers, supervisors, and, yes, for CSRs on the front-line. Read the book and listen to the "heartbeat" of a very special author and champion of the importance of "getting jazzed about your CSRs and quality in your call center."

My son Kevin is a pretty good baseball player. From the time he was very young, we taught him to hit left-handed although he throws the ball right-handed. I love watching left-handed batters swing at the baseball. They seem to have an advantage facing right-handed hitters, and they are a step closer to first base. It looks confusing because he throws right-handed, and you just expect him to be a right-handed batter. You wouldn't be able to tell the difference until you saw him get up to the batter's box.

Like left-handed and right-handed baseball players, the business world struggles with mixing two different types of players. These are intellectuals and warriors.

Intellectuals are a different breed. They seem to be the ones that really understand the "whys" of business. They are well read, have a firm understanding of history, and always seem to have an opinion—if not the right answer—about the future. You know the type. If there is a new book, they have read it; a new theory, they have contemplated it; a new industry, they have reviewed it and already invested in it.

The warriors, on the other hand, like action. They want to be in the game, making something happen. They use their gut instincts. They get wrapped up in what's going on today, and they are good at responding quickly and accurately to the situation that presents itself.

The challenge is that warriors are usually too busy making history to spend anytime reading about it, and intellectuals are too busy thinking about the game to ever really play. The reality is that we need both types of people to make a great company. Action, planning, and information make for a very powerful combination. Are you a warrior or an intellectual? Like most of us, you probably answered, "I'm a little of both."

Call Centers are a "little of both." They require an enormous amount of planning and produce an amazing amount of information, yet they spend each day, hour, and minute reacting to the constant changes and challenges of their customers. When you walk into a call center, you can immediately see what is important and figure out the strategy for this part of the business. What you see are usually large rooms, lots of cubicles, some sort of control center, and people talking on the telephone—everywhere. The priority is very simple: customers. You can feel the focus on customers. You can see the attention to volume. You can see the commitment and investment in people, technology, and process.

This business is first and foremost about people. People are everything in this business. The premise of call centers is based on a very scary people proposition. We take our most valuable asset—our customers—and connect them with our newest, most inexperienced employees, (more than 30 percent are new each year) and expect world-class customer service. Sound crazy? Welcome to our world!

With over 60,000 call centers in the United States alone, the quality of these centers runs the gamut from world-class to pathetic—or to put it much more kindly, from professional to amateur. The warrior side of me would say, "Danger, Will Robinson! Start paying attention to your call centers! Do you even know you have a call center? Hello! Is anyone home? Do you see how big of an asset you have here? Executives, do you know how much information is available about your customers and your business? Do you know the impact your center could have on your company? Can you see what a world-class quality program can do for your competitive advantage?"

Customer service and client retention are the priorities of the market place! The ability to acquire and keep clients in a cost effective way will be the difference between the winners and losers. It doesn't take a computer scientist to see the priorities of the market today. It is crystal clear to me.

My intellectual side would put it another way. It would explain that my goal—make that my quest—is to make sure that every call center agent, manager, CEO, and stockholder of the 60,000-plus call centers out there today gets jazzed about their current and future centers. For over 20 years, call centers have been one of the best examples of the information and service economy. There is much to learn and improve as we discover more about this wonderful customer tool. You can improve your service level. You can use your call center as a strategic asset. The decisions and strategies that you put in place to measure and improve quality can positively affect your bottom line.

Having the privilege of being in a market called call centers has influenced my perspective and jaded my view. This book includes many of my perspectives on people, process, quality monitoring, technology, and performance. I have been in the call center market for more than 20 years. I began as a salesperson in New York City and had the privilege of being an executive in a new industry and market that we had developed called performance management, or quality monitoring. I have been involved with the entire alphabet soup such as UCD, ACD, CTI, VRU, IVR, and of course CRM, just to name a few. As a result of my experience, I have arrived at several interesting insights into this industry. I have also developed my personal perspective on business, which is both passionate and direct. It is my goal to share these insights and perspectives with you.

In this book, we will focus on the different types of people in the call center, spending time to understand the different types of representatives as well as the supervisors and executives. Call centers are ultimately about people and how to help those people do the very best job they can for you and your customers. We will examine the age-old dilemma of how well versus how much. Finally, we will move further into the 21st century and look at new ways to use technology and new applications that can help you find a competitive edge in the marketplace.

As you read this book, you will notice two interesting features. The first is an occasional reference to a movie quote. I have learned that bits of knowledge can be found everywhere—especially in movies. I have provided a few of my favorites for you.

The other feature is a Wrap-Up at the end of each chapter, similar to the wrap-up that agents use when they make calls. This feature is meant to reinforce the main ideas that you should take away from this book. It is your job to put them to use.

Whether you have 400 or 4 people providing sales or service over the phone or Web, you can learn from this book. You may actually have a call center, and you don't even know it. If you are an executive who has noted how wonderful your call center is in your yearly report but don't know a thing about it or appreciate its value, you are in the right place. If you are a newly hired agent who is just entering the industry, this book can help you. Whatever your position or experience, the truths about call centers that I have learned over the years will hopefully strike a chord with you and encourage you to continue your quest for excellence.

Maybe, just maybe, it will bring out a little more warrior or intellectual in you and help you to be a major part of a world-class call center.

Now let's get to work.

Section One

Discovering How We Got Where We Are Today

CHAPTER 1: THE TRUE NATURE OF CALL CENTERS

The Four-Minute Market

- Thank you for calling ABC Corporation.

- Press 1 for service.

- Press 2 for sales.

- Press 25 for all other questions.

- All our agents are busy; please hold for the next available representative.

- Your call may be monitored or recorded for quality purposes.

These statements are a part of our everyday lives. Our friends, family, fellow church members, and business associates all work in call centers around the world. Today, 800 numbers now include 888 numbers and other additional number combinations to meet the growing need for support and services. Technology, people, and process are all meshed together to deliver products and services around the globe. It is an amazing marketplace that has been around for a quarter of century. The market continues to grow and add new capability and responsibility.

The call center industry is like no other. This market is built on a premise that a company usually has less than 240 seconds to solve a problem or gain an opportunity, either over the phone, on the Web, or with e-mail, using for the most part entry-level people in a situation with a 30 percent turnover rate. We have to create, delight, and retain customers in less time that it takes to boil an egg. We have to do it millions of times a year and with quality. In this industry, one extra second with a customer or client could be worth hundreds of thousands of dollars.

> This industry has to create, delight, and retain customers in less time than it takes to boil an egg.

3

Our industry accomplishes this task, for the most part, never meeting the customers face-to-face, never knowing when they will arrive or when they will leave. We do this with very little fanfare, and for many years, we did it with little technology and few standards. This incredible industry is performing miracles in the business world. Unfortunately most leaders and executives don't recognize the value it possesses nor appreciate the contribution that their call centers make.

The lifeline of a call center is its people and the processes that are built around them. The landscape and expectations of call centers has changed over the years. Nowhere is that more apparent than in the persistent battle between selling and servicing customers.

Sales Versus Service

Having been in the industry for 20 years, I understand the basic dilemma between sales and service. I too have struggled with finding the perfect balance. I knew I was born to sell from the very first time that I sold candy for the Ledyard, Connecticut Boys Little League. I love it; I get it. I also learned early about territory management and distribution when I figured out that my father could sell more at work than I could in the neighborhood! Customer service, on the other hand, has taken some time to warm up to over the years.

My parents would not tell you that I was born to serve by any means. I tried to avoid chores and work at all costs. During the summer, I was very sure I was allergic to grass and in the fall, leaves. In the winter, my back was one driveway of snow away from collapsing. So much for trying to avoid work. My first job was as a janitor in a church, then dishwasher, highway road crew, submarine torpedo machinist, computer tape jockey, another dishwasher run, usher in a movie theater (I saw The Empire Strikes Back 67 times!), then positions in sales, management, product management, marketing, and finally, President, and CEO.

I have learned over the years that customer service is a privilege and an honor. There is nothing that gets me more jazzed than to serve people. I love it. I also have a passion for selling. The great news is that in the call center market, every call or Web interaction is a sales and service opportunity. Together, they present an amazing challenge with incredible rewards for doing it successfully. I am convinced that the great call centers and service people really enjoy what they are doing. They really like to help people and make a difference. The desire to serve is important to your success.

4

If the first sentence of the last paragraph just made you cringe, you are going to have a problem being in the sales or service business. However, all hope is not lost. You too can find a balance between sales and customer service. The trick is to do both of them well and neither of them in isolation.

> The desire to serve is important to your success.

The challenge of selling over the phone is complicated enough without adding the burden of customer service. Everyone knows that these are very different skills in many instances. The difficulty of making a call center sale is complicated by the fact that the transaction is very fast, and there is very little time to establish a relationship. The conversation itself is the employee's work product, and the sales are the result.

On the plus side, call center sales usually arrive much more qualified than a normal face-to-face sales cycle. The opportunity to make contact is free (with the use of 800 numbers). Potential customers know exactly why they are coming to you, and the investment they have to make to "try out your store" is minimal. In many instances, Web traffic is even easier. Easier also can mean less commitment. On the negative side, less commitment by the prospective customer means it is easier for them to go somewhere else.

The key factor is that the advent of Customer Relationship Management (CRM) makes us take seriously the selling and servicing of customers over the phone. Customer Relationship Management has many different and diverse definitions. My definition is the business process of interacting and growing together with your customer throughout their entire experience with your company. This is not foo-foo double-speak. We are trying to sell, deliver, and service our customers. They are trying to buy, receive, and make use of our products and service. The interaction or relationship is defined over months, years, and decades and is viewed collectively and rather than as individual transactions.

A Balancing Act

For years, it was easy for call centers to use two separate phone numbers for sales and service. Call centers were at the very front of a number of isolated transactions. One number was for sales. Another less accessible and usually less responsive number was for customer service. It was viewed as a separated transaction for the delivery, installation, repair, etc. Each part was not connected and most certainly not connected to the original call. Many companies today still use this process. Other companies have hidden this quagmire by allowing for one-number presence. Customers are automatically switched to another department for service support once they make contact. This provides the beginning of connection.

CRM drives us to recognize that virtually every call or transaction from its very inception is both a sales and service call. Every sales call has an opportunity to provide service. That's easy to understand. On the flip side, every service call presents an opportunity to sell. This is what the promise of CRM really is. We can enhance our relationship with our customers by using every contact and deliverable to further the success and profitability of our client relationship, which hopefully will last forever! Every transaction that we have with the customer is a selling opportunity if we are focused on the lifetime value of the customer and not just the transaction. Every action helps us build a long-term deeper relationship.

> Every call or transaction is both a sales and service call.

Knowing the When's and Why's

Let's take a more provocative and different look at the sales and service process. One of the best places to look at sales is on the sales that you lose. Like most areas of life, we seem to learn more from our failures than we do from our successes. This is no different in the sales arena. If you follow the sales process closely, you will find that one of the critical misunderstandings of the sales win-loss evaluation is the total focus first on *why* the sale was lost. Much time and effort is placed on trying to find out the "real" reason why the customer didn't go with you. Much time and effort is spent trying to find the reason *why* the sale was lost.

I believe that the more important component of a lost sale is *when* you lost the deal. If you understand when you lost the deal, you can save the most valuable asset of a salesperson—your time. Sales time is crucial to success in any business. We fight and scratch for more sales time in front of our customers. There is an added benefit of focusing on the "when" versus the "why." If you can find out when you lost the sale, you can more easily find out what the reasons were. It is a faster way to the "why". Knowing the time immediately eliminates many areas of your business and helps you focus on the real reasons you lost.

> Much time and effort is spent trying to find the reason why the sale was lost. The more important component of a lost sale is when you lost the deal.

When you transfer this sales theory over to the call center and mix in the importance of CRM and servicing the customer into this "four-minute whirlwind," you get quite a chaotic mess. If you go back to the first paragraph of this chapter, we state that a typical call center transaction:

- usually has less than 240 seconds to solve a problem or gain an opportunity

- must create, delight, and retain customers

- while never meeting the customers, never knowing when they will arrive or when they will leave

- must be done millions of times a year with quality.

A call center is all about time. Our customers view of "why" we win or lose can be anywhere in the relationship, not just the transaction on the phone or Web. Remember when we say "lose" that is both real business today and long-term opportunity that can be ten or one thousand times more than our original interaction.

Can we build a long-term relationship with clients over the telephone and the Web without servicing the customer throughout the interaction? Is it possible to take care of the sale and shift them to someone else and fully expect them to become a lifetime customer? The answer has to be "no." In today' environment, the relationship transcends the phone call. The all-important "when" can occur at any time during the relationship.

We can do many brilliant things in the span of four minutes or less. There are call centers all over the world working magic with their clients day in and day out. If we could have stayed in our cocoon of just the call center, we could spend our days fighting over whether to service or sell our customers with the same people or the same numbers. The problem is that CRM came along. We are no longer isolated. We can't take all the credit or the blame. We are just one area—an extremely important and underutilized area, I might add, of the entire offering of the company. Our interaction can help our company provide new offerings, upgrade and enhance our relationships with our customers, and make a difference down the supply chain that we could never have dreamed of before.

Three Basic Elements

If you measure the amount of investment and time put into preparing for those four-minute interactions, you would think that the job of a call center is impossible. The challenge to create, delight, and retain transcends every area of the company. CRM can sound complicated, but at its core, it is selling and servicing the customer. It's just all done at the same time. Perhaps we can create a new word like "selervicing" or "salervice." Great selling is inevitably great servicing. More importantly, great servicing opens door for great selling.

What is really exciting is that as we come to grips with these changes, it drives us back to three key important factors. These are:

- people
- quality
- technology.

Each one of these is a crucial factor in attempting to service and sell our customers. Each one of these plays a critical role in the successful relationship with our customers and clients. Each one works with another to make the process successful.

We will spend a lot time in this book focusing on these three areas and how we can better understand the relationship among them. We will find that a call center is one of the very best places to learn about our customers, our company, and our economy.

WRAP-UP

- Call Centers perform four-minute miracles daily all around the world.

- Sales and service are amazingly intertwined if they are both done well.

- "When you lose a sale" is a higher priority first over "why you lost a sale."

- CRM has forever changed the landscape of call centers. We are no longer isolated.

The Advent of Call Centers

After several thousand years of believing that the Sun revolved around the Earth, Copernicus finally convinced the world the Earth revolved around the Sun.

Similarly, for years we have believed that the call center was at the back end of business, and it was always the last to know everything. Ten years ago people didn't even know what a call center was. They didn't even know if they had one! Call centers were the place that everything happened "to." They were cost centers, problem centers, and black holes for spending money with no upside.

The term call center came from either Jim Carreker, founder of Aspect Telecommunications, or Gordon MacPhearson, founder of the Incoming Calls Management Institute. It might have been Jim's napkin and Gordon's handwriting or the other way around. Either way, they are both giants in the history of call centers.

Jim entered the call center industry through Datapoint Corporation. He then started Aspect Telecommunications with a stop at Dataquest. His Automatic Call Distribution System, which was built with an integrated voice mail system, took the industry by storm. Gordon MacPhearson started the Incoming Calls Management Institute. I had the privilege of going to his very first seminar. He was one of the original founders of the ICCM show. His former business partner Brad Cleveland now ably runs ICMI.

Two Distinct Purposes

Since the beginning, call centers have been divided into two distinct areas: revenue generation and revenue protection. The very first known call center was Continental Airlines. It was a revenue generation site and was designed to make money by taking airline reservations. (Note: Call centers for years have called the people who answer the phone "agents." This was the term that airlines used to refer to their telephone representatives.)

A revenue protection site was one that provided customer service but didn't "sell" anything. I don't know what the first revenue protection center was. From the world's perspective, however, I think the GE Answer Center would be its choice. GE was one of the first, if not the first, companies to really focus on a call center being the place to get your answers and receive superior service. GE put call centers in the public view.

Over the years, there have been far more revenue protection than revenue generation call centers. Customer Relationship Management (CRM), which we discussed in the last chapter, is changing the focus of many of these revenue protection centers to revenue generation as well. Until now, the call center seemed to revolve around everything else. It was a necessary cost evil.

The Emergence of Alphabet Soup Technology

The reality is that the concept of call centers didn't get off to a great start. Some of the very early images of call centers were either telephone operator rooms, sweat shop telephone offices, and even worse, obnoxious telemarketing shops. Most people's perspectives were skewed by poor initial interactions with call centers. They didn't understand that there was a new industry brewing.

> Call centers were first viewed as cost centers, problem centers, and black holes for spending money.

In the early days of call centers, there was Rockwell International and no one else. I say no one else because Rockwell had something called a Stand-Alone Automatic Call Distributor (ACD). This meant that its only task was moving large volumes of inbound, homogeneous calls to anonymous agents.

As more call centers entered the scene, so did new technologies. Some used Private Branch Exchanges (PBXs) and network systems with a feature to move high volumes of calls. At one time in the late 70s, call centers used Automatic Call Sequencers, Uniform Call Distributors (UCD), as well as PBXs.

Datapoint joined the scene in the late 70s as another player in the market for inbound telephone calling as a stand-alone product called the Infoswitch ACD. The difference between an ACD and the others was that an ACD sent the call to the longest-waiting agent, allowing even distribution. UCD had used a top-down rotation, so there was always a hot seat. All the calls would rotate down the list of agents. This meant that agent number one was always offered the call first. If not already busy, that agent always got the next call. The same thing occurred next for agent two, etc.

At this same time, the outbound telemarketing and collections companies were starting to grow as well. This is where some of the bad press came from in the early days. What is fascinating is that the very first Predictive Dialer was one of the very best productivity telephone improvements ever developed. Stories of 300 to 400 percent improvement over manual dialing were commonplace.

Early Efforts to Monitor

Recording phone calls has been around for a very long time as well. The list of loggers and recorders is as long as my arm. Originally developed for 911 systems and financial transactions, the very first quality management system specifically for the random monitoring of calls didn't go in effect until 1993.

The first quality monitoring system, by Teknekron Infoswitch Corporation, was installed at U.S. Surgical Corporation of Connecticut, now a part of Tyco International. Witness Systems, Roswell, Georgia, had been doing screen recording for training purposes during the early 90s in a small group of companies. Their first client was American Express Corporation.

What spurred the quality management business was the ability to double the amount of monitoring while cutting the time needed by 50 percent, with no increase in personnel.

The connection between quality and productivity in business has been around for a very long time. One of the earliest uses of measuring the productivity and quality together for quality management purposes in a call center was done by Dr. Gene Swystun, formerly of Teknekron Infoswitch Corporation. Some of the charts you see vendors promote today came from his original work.

The New Image of Call Centers

Call centers have come a long way since these early beginnings. They are no longer at the back end of the business. CRM has recognized the critical component of the call center and the key role that it plays in maximizing the lifetime value of a customer. It is not

13

only the center of the service and sales offering but also a key area for obtaining information.

> Call centers hold a vast array of valuable information about our products, services, costs, and most importantly, customer preferences and needs.

There is a story of a man who stood on top of a building. He looked to his left and then to his right. He noticed that it was the same distance to his left as it was to his right. He concluded that he was standing at the center of the universe.

That's how call centers in world-class companies are viewed today. If you stood in the middle of any world-class customer service company today, the call center would be at the "center of their strategy" for supporting and servicing customers. Customer contact centers—as call centers are increasingly referred to today as they incorporate more than just telephone communications—are now the "center of the universe" of customer service and customer contact. This is where the important transactions take place and where the critical information is gathered for running a successful company.

We in the industry know that we are important, but sometimes we drift back to the past. This year I had the opportunity to go to ICCM, which is one of the industry's largest tradeshows. At the show, several managers received an award for Call Center Manager of the Year.

One of the recipients from Australia told a humorous story about another award he had received. He explained that it was a toilet brush to help him remember that his job was cleaning up everyone else's mess. The cool thing is that perhaps at one time we all would have received a toilet brush. Today, however, we are at the front end of the CRM chain, which is critical first step in achieving a lifetime relationship with our clients. Perhaps next year he will get a "chrome handle" to better describe where we are in the process!

Toilet Brush or Center of the Universe? Center of the Universe has a nice ring to it!

WRAP-UP

- The beginning of the term *call center* can be credited to Jim Carreker and Gordon MacPhearson.

- Call centers have historically been divided between revenue generation and revenue protection, but this is changing.

- Call centers are increasingly being viewed as the important hub of information within the company.

CHAPTER 3: TRENDS THAT HAVE MADE HISTORY

The Four Greatest Changes in Call Centers

The new image of call centers did not emerge overnight. The leap from being a black hole to the "center of the universe" took some time—20 years, as a matter of fact.

We have had many significant changes and turns in the customer service and call center industry in the last 20 years. None in and of themselves have single handedly turned the industry. I do feel that as we stand back and look, several important changes come to mind. I have identified four of these key changes and trends that have brought us where we are today. They are:

- the invention of the Interactive Voice Response Unit
- the introduction of the universal agent
- advancements in desktop technology
- the emergence of the call center agent as a career choice.

This is by no means an exhaustive list, but I believe these developments have had the greatest impact on the quality and performance of call centers.

Interactive Voice Response Unit (IVR) or Voice Response Unit (VRU)

The Advantages of IVR

The IVR/VRU is one of the single most important technological changes to take place in the call center so far. A VRU is a telephony device that uses touch-tone inputs by a telephone, which interacts with a computer to provide a canned response to the caller.

In the beginning there were no IVRs. Every call had to be handled by a representative. This meant that every call was handled by a resource (a person) that was pretty much the same cost. There was no alternative. No matter how long or short or mundane the call was, a person handled it.

17

Call centers were originally invented to get a lower-paying person to handle these mundane and simple calls that had to be handled. Upon the introduction of IVR, this equation changed. When IVR technology entered the marketplace, it had many attractive attributes. It was less expensive ($2,500 to $5,500 per port versus someone's salary and benefit package). In addition, it was able to work 24-hours-a-day 365-days-a-year, did not get sick, was always accurate, and had no desire to unionize! Each of these attributes made call centers very attractive.

These units started out taking the simplest calls. The definition of simple has changed over time. In the beginning, the most common transaction was an account balance call.

The result has been phenomenal. For example, for many in the retail banking industry today, more than 70 percent of calls are handled by IVR. Most other industries handle at least 20 percent of their calls this way.

- What is the percentage for your industry?
- How close are you to it?
- If you are behind, you are at an extreme disadvantage.

If you are in an industry where IVR is not prevalent or your leaders "don't like voicemail," you had better be prepared to change.

> To have a call center today and not have some sort of IVR is strange and unnatural.

New Challenges that IVR Brings

Even with all the wonderful things that the IVR does, it still creates a problem. The IVR naturally takes all of the simpler calls because these are the ones that can be automated. This is great and a tremendous cost-saver. However, IVR is taking away the simpler calls. This puts more pressure on your hiring models and your training goals and process. This problem is compounded by the fact that companies are constantly searching for ways to add new types of services and transactions to the center. Now, your entry-level personnel must handle more complicated calls and a growing number of different transactions. Measuring responses and attempting to calibrate the work effort is much more difficult.

18

There is a new problem. The remaining calls that aren't handled by the IVR are now much more complicated. This means that the remaining interactions we have available to our newest and least experienced employees are more difficult. This may seem like a very small issue, but it is cornerstone to your challenge today in providing customer service to your clients.

Let me state this another way. For years we have been hiring entry-level people to handle entry-level tasks. With the advent of IVR and the ever-growing speech recognition taking over many of these entry-level type calls, we are at risk of hiring entry-level people to handle complicated, higher-level problems instead of entry-level problems.

IVR's will get smarter. Companies like Nuance Communications, Menlo Park, California, are striving to make the technology stretch into more complex calls. The very real advent of voice recognition will continue to make applications more available to voice response. This will speed up the types and availability of services.

The potential for voice recognition is unparalleled in the industry. If you have ever experienced these devices, you can see the potential. Recently, I was able to complete an entire transaction for a phone number search without an operator. American Airlines has used the technology for gate and arrival information. It is still too slow most of the time and sometimes aggravating to communicate, but the upside is enormous.

> The potential for voice recognition is unparalleled in the industry.

IVR is universally known as the technology we love to hate. We see the benefits, but for the most part, we really would rather speak to a human being. As great as an IVR is, it's not very good at empathy. With companies like Nuance making them smarter and more conversational, it shouldn't be long before they start saying things like; "I feel your pain" and "You would really look good in that red scarf!"

Until that time we will continue to put pressure on the greatest strength and weakness of our centers—the agents.

The Universal Agent

The Pros and Cons

A second important change that emerged was the universal agent. Initially, a universal agent was someone who could perform more than one type of transaction. In other words, these agents were better able to handle many different types of calls.

Currently, there is an interesting dichotomy between where the industry is going with the concept of universal agents and the technology that these agents use.

For cost reasons, the industry naturally wants agents to be able to answer as many different types of calls as possible. The more calls they can handle, the fewer the number of people the call centers need to dedicate to different areas. The challenge is finding the mix between accuracy, quality, and cost.

> Universal agents are trained to be better able to handle many different types of calls.

Originally centers were based on anonymous callers going to homogeneous agents. You had a bunch of callers that the company did not know prior to contact going to one pool of agents who were equipped to handle all calls. The benefits of this type of arrangement are important to consider. First, our pool of available people to service the clients is bigger. This means less cost and fewer resources necessary to solve a problem. Just think about the lines at the bank and the benefits of feeding from one line into a number of tellers who can solve any problem. The more universal the agent, the more resources we can make available to solve the problem. Second, we trained everyone the same, and we had one group to handle all problems. We also were not concerned with handling customers differently.

Technology and customer needs changed this arrangement. Companies began providing different queues for customers to call into. They used Direct Inward Dial (DID) to supply separate numbers for specific agents or groups. This meant a different level of service, sometimes better and sometimes worse. It also meant smaller queues.

This created a need for routing to different queues and the ability to go back and forth between groups. In this scenario, Group A could handle their calls plus be a backup for Group B. These agents became known as "universal" because they could handle more than one queue of calls. The more types of queues they could handle, the more universal they were.

Mixing Inbound and Outbound Calls

Some call centers, for instance, have tried to blend inbound and outbound calling. This has met with limited success. The technology to do this is available, yet the internal customer processes and culture have lagged behind. We can mix and merge the inbound and outbound experience. It can be very complicated, but it can be done. The problem is that the agent has to switch from one to the other. This is a hard transition to make. For one call, the agent is taking an inbound customer service call. On the very next call, that same agent is put into a predictive dialer.

A predictive dialer makes a large amount of outbound calls and predicts an agent being able to talk to the customer. Have you ever heard an announcement when someone called you that said, "Please wait for a very important message?" Several seconds later, someone came on the phone and tried to sell you something. If so, that was probably a predictive dialer that aggressively got ahead of the people available to talk.

In many instances, the agent has a tough time switching from an inbound service call to an outbound sales call. Inbound and outbound universal agents have been done and done successfully but have not experienced the success originally desired.

Another ironic twist is that today's technology allows call center managers to route calls based on skills. "Skills-based routing" was designed to put the best resource in the right place at the right time. (For more on skills-based routing, see Chapter 28.) However, this can hinder the efficiency of the universal agent and restrict the opportunity of those who are trying to become more complete universal agents. You can see the predicament. We need skill-based agents to solve our most difficult and complicated problems. However, every time we segment the interaction, we reduce the size of our queues, making our call center less efficient and more costly.

The Changing Role of Universal Agents

In the past, universal agents focused predominantly on the different types of transactions that took place over the phone. An agent was said to be universal if he or she could handle service and sales or claims and customer service, printers and CPUs.

The term *universal agent* has now been extended to include the medium of the transaction. Today, a universal agent may be an agent that can handle voice, Web chat, and e-mail.

This change means new training is required. All of a sudden, we now have to worry about grammar and the agents' ability to write. The other very critical part of this equation is that with more written interactions between companies and customers, our legal risks increase as well. What we say, even if recorded, is more complicated and can be ineffective to work with in court. What we write in documents like e-mails are much easier to enter as evidence. Just ask Bill Gates!

This desire for agents to do more has put additional pressure on the quality function and the training area. The challenge is threefold: to increase the capacity of what the agent can perform, while increasing his or her skills and while reducing turnover.

> Today, a universal agent may be an agent that can handle voice, Web chat, and e-mail.

Universal agents, by whatever definition you choose, continue to change the landscape of the call center. We put a lot of pressure and responsibility on the agent. Their workload becomes more complicated with each new year. One of the key ways we overcome these new challenges is with new technology at the desktop.

Desktop Technology

Computer Telephone Integration

To combat the stress of more complicated calls and the growing pressure to service and support many different types of interactions, companies have turned to technology at the desktop.

It may seem crazy, but a few years ago and for some major call centers today, there were no PCs at the desktop. Companies were restricted to their mainframe applications. As time progressed, companies installed PCs at the desktop, and the opportunity for improved service grew immediately. Computer Telephone Integration (CTI), the combination of computer and telephony capabilities, was one of the first technologies that emerged, and with it came more tools and resources for the agent.

One hardware change was the elimination of the telephone. Many centers have a combined computer and telephone within their PCs. This has allowed the agent to focus on the desktop and has streamlined many of the features and capabilities of the phone set.

One key capability has been "screen pops." This enables the agent to be prepared for the client before the call arrives. This has also saved up to 15 seconds of the transaction on the front end of the call in some instances. However, companies need to be careful in this area. There is nothing more aggravating than participating in a screen pop call and then having to repeat the same information again because the agent didn't get the data.

Opportunities Through Software and the Web

New power at the desktop has brought forth Web chat, e-mail, CRM software and hardware, as well as many other technology solutions that have made the agent more capable. This technological power is right where it needs to be—at the fingertips of the agents. It is producing great results.

Customer Interaction Management Software

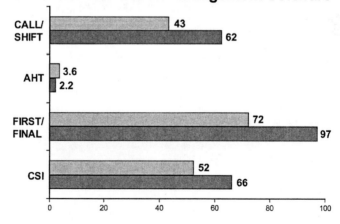

In this graph from BenchmarkPortal Inc., you can see the effect that advanced technology can have on a call center. The areas in dark gray represent those companies that have made an investment in desktop technology and customer interaction capability. You can see an improvement in every area where the technology has been deployed. For those not familiar with the terms, they are Calls per Shift, Average Handle Time, First Call Resolution, and Caller Satisfaction Index.

Companies that once had only dumb terminals continue to invest in state-of-the-art personal computers with large screens and new, easy graphical user interfaces. They have increased the quality of the customer interactions by putting more information and power at the fingertips of the agent.

Movie Quote:
"I think we need a bigger boat."
— Roy Schneider in *Jaws* [1]

Personal Comment: Many years ago, I needed a rake to gather the leaves that had fallen on my lawn. I went to a local hardware store and purchased the cheapest rake I could find. I then spent the next hour laboring over the leaves in my yard. Later, my neighbor came out and started raking his leaves. He had a smile on his face, and he moved much quicker than I did; yet he was 20 years older than I was. I asked to borrow his rake, and it was an amazing difference. I realized that I was suffering because I had purchased a poor quality tool to do the job.

Business Application: Many different technologies currently exist that are designed to monitor and increase the productivity of call centers. If you are not utilizing the latest technological developments, you need a bigger boat.

Web chat is an excellent example of how bringing more power to the desktop of a service and sales person can make a difference. Web chat enables customers to communicate with the company using an interface that not only allows them to communicate in real time but also to collaborate as well. In this circumstance, the agent can push pages to the customer and help them navigate through the Web site. This type of power enhances their interaction and improves the level of service and number of options available to the customer.

> Today's technological power is right where it needs to be—at the fingertips of the agents.

New innovations such as Voice over IP will also benefit from increased power at the desktop. This technology allows voice traffic and Web traffic to occur simultaneously. The above-mentioned service scenario would be additionally improved by the ability to talk through your personal computer to the customer while taking advantage of the improved interaction over the Web.

Voice over IP is just a small step to video over Web, where we can talk and see each other. In a business environment, the application can be varied and there is much upside. However, it will be interesting to watch whether companies really want you to see whom you are talking to and who is serving you. Do you think that nose rings, tattoos, and lip piercing will improve or detract from the sales and service process?

The desktop will continue to see more advancement and improvement in the coming years. We measure our success by the balance between quality and productivity. The desktop is one area that will continue to play an important role in this delicate balance. The desktop technology can have a bigger impact when the people operating the technology are well trained and experienced. This has been a significant change in call centers.

Call Center Agent as Professional/Career Choice

Potential for Promotion

One of the most exciting new trends is that the position of customer service/call center representative is quickly becoming a career in and of itself. Today, many companies use a call center position as a starting point in the business. Once bright call center agents are knowledgeable about the ways of the company, they are moved into other more "important" departments where they can further their careers. This is both a strength and a weakness.

There is no better place to learn about the company than in the call center. It touches every area of the business. However, by moving your most productive employees out of the call center, you increase the number of new and inexperienced agents. This creates the situation of constantly matching your company's most valuable assets—your customers—with your most inexperienced employees.

Education for Call Center Agents

Universities all across the nation have added curriculum on customer service and call center agent training. Junior colleges have developed courses on the skills necessary to be a successful customer

25

service representative. Northwest Vista Junior College in San Antonio has technology that allows students to participate in computer simulations in which students can practice being call center agents. Purdue University continues to maintain a leadership position in the call center arena.

> The position of customer service/call center representative is quickly becoming a career in and of itself.

The connection to education must not stop at the university level. We can see the large amount of employees in call centers that come directly out of our nation's high schools. Representing over three percent of the workforce in 2001, call centers make up an even higher percentage of first time entry-level jobs in the country. This fact is important to our nation's success. We need to move more aggressively to start training programs in our high schools as well.

Career Possibilities

The very real existence of call center agents working from their homes makes the success of this profession far reaching to our economy. The economic, environmental, and relational benefits of an additional profession that can work out of the home are substantial. Call centers have the technology, the volume, and the wide range of skills needed to make an impact around the country. As the demographics of workforce change in the next 10 to 20 years, this flexibility will prove beneficial. The company gets better access to talented people, reduced cost, more flexible hours, and longer tenured employees.

Call centers also include more that just calls. The advent of Web chat and e-mail is a fast-growing function of call centers. Many of the career opportunities available in servicing and supporting customers are becoming even more exciting.

Today, businesses are recognizing that a call center representative can make a career out of the position. Call centers are more confident about providing additional training and skills to help agents become more valuable to the organization. Their value can be seen in higher salary, position, benefits, and visibility for their contributions.

There are hundreds of individual circumstances and changes that have affected the call center, or customer contact, industry. These four trends have not only affected the past but will also affect the future of centers in the years to come.

WRAP-UP

- Interactive Voice Response Units are essential for success in a call center.

- As technology increases, the role of the universal agent will become more complex.

- New technologies can put power at the agents' fingertips.

- Many people are now choosing call center agent as their career choice.

CHAPTER 4: INTO THE INFORMATION AGE

A Changing Economy

Not only are call centers now recognized as the "center of the universe" in many companies, they may also be a model of the universe still to come. More than any other industry, call centers provide a fascinating reflection of the changing business climate of the United States and the rest of the world.

> Call centers clearly echo the changes and excitement of the new digital economy that is upon us.

The concept of phone support, while a part of our very culture, is sometimes considered old hat and past news. Believe it or not, the phone is continually on the verge of replacement by futurists and techno-experts who seek alternatives for connecting with our clients. Our first reality is that we seem to have an insatiable appetite to communicate. No matter what new medium of communication we bring forward (i.e., voice mail, e-mail, video conferencing), we seem to keep making phone calls.

What is really intriguing is that call centers are one of the most obvious and time-tested examples of the impact and potential of the Information Age. That's right. We have right in front of us real live data about technology and the impact it can have on our commerce today. There is much to be learned from the experience of call centers in the last 20 years and many principles to be applied for business and management in the new millennium.

Call centers represent almost three percent of the U.S. workforce and a significantly larger percentage of the entry-level positions in this country. More significantly, call centers may represent up to ten percent of the Fortune 1000 college graduates who enter the workforce each year. The shift to a service economy has no better growth partner and model than the call center industry.

Think about it. We have an industry that:

- has experienced monumental technology change
- includes both a non-educated technical workforce and now a very sophisticated technical workforce
- provides worldwide business experience, and most importantly, has over 20 years of data.

Let's look at some of the areas that many companies today have experienced in their call centers and see if you haven't heard of them being the challenges and solutions of tomorrow.

Worldwide Enterprise

As the world expands into a global economy, worldwide communications will become vital to all businesses. The hub of these communications will be call centers. Most companies committed to global support already have call centers around the globe. Today, call centers are some of the first investments made by multinational companies to establish worldwide presence and new relationships. They continue to grow in all parts of the world, bringing technology and white-collar service positions to emerging countries around the globe.

Connection to the Customer

Another way that call centers reflect the new economy is through the emphasis on customer service. The Information Age has made consumers more knowledgeable and more demanding. All companies must focus on providing quality service in order to meet the changing needs of their customers.

The unending needs of the consumer for service and communication are readily seen in the increasing number of ways that a call center can be contacted. In each instance of increased communication such as voice response, e-mail, Web chat, video, and the telephone, real-live contact continues to grow and serve the marketplace.

Call centers also allow opportunities for self-service. Automation of simpler tasks continues to change the landscape of the call center. Voice Response and the Internet have played a dramatic role in changing the requirements of the people that work in call centers and the customers. Nowhere has the business concept of self-service played a more major role than in call centers.

Recognition of Around the Clock Support

One of the key initiatives of worldwide call centers was to provide around-the-clock support for products and services. Today, 24x7 support, 365 days a year is standard within the call center industry. This type of nonstop service and support is necessary for the new economy.

Staffing and scheduling of white collar workers has been enhanced and improved. The sending home of people when there isn't enough work has been a standard in the call center industry for two decades. This type of real-time control of workforce management provides a competitive advantage in the new economy.

Optimal schedules that transcend the normal workweek and recognize the seven-day needs of the consumer are commonplace. Forecasting schedules of an economy that can't be predictable about their arrival or requirements driven by geography, the market place or individual preferences are the fears of the business world. This is commonplace in call centers.

Performance Measurement

Call centers may very well be the very first validation of the Information Age. Did we get the benefit of what we spent? We have the measurement tools, and we have the experience. The advantage is that we can measure the entire interaction in the call center. This type of measurement and experience will be important as technology moves into others parts of the enterprise.

Performance measurement has been a part of call centers for over 20 years. Call centers measure employee performance to the second. Quality is mined for agent performance improvement as well as key client and product information and improvement.

Quality analysis goes beyond just the number of failures of the transaction. It provides companies a real focus on the relationship outcomes of the interactions and the impact on the company and the customer.

Employee Relations

Call centers also serve as models for the changing face of employee relations. Most call centers employ part-time staff whose demographics cover the aging population as well as the new entrants into the white-collar service industry. A 30 percent turnover rate is the norm in call centers. Our new economy is fast approaching the recognition that the 20-year employee is a distant remnant of the past.

> Call centers serve as models for the changing face of employee relations.

Entry-level, lower paying, white-collar jobs are the standard for call centers. The entry point for call centers requires computer skills. Computer skills are also a requirement for the new economy.

The entry-level position of a call center has continually increased the amount of tasks and responsibilities of the agents. This is being done through:

- enhancements in technology
- additional business requirements
- a desire to keep costs in line.

Future advancements in these areas will be needed in call centers—and most other businesses—as we move into the new millennium.

An entire book could be written on just this chapter alone. In the following chapters, I will continue to show you just how important your call center can be to you. The information is there for you to use. Take some advice: "Carpe diem-ata," or in English, "Seize the data!"

WRAP-UP

- Call centers mirror many of the changes that are taking place in the economy.

- The focus on customer service in call centers will be an important facet of business in the future.

- Call centers have set a standard for 24-hour customer support.

- Like almost all industries, entry-level positions in the call center will continue to require new and advanced skills.

Section Two

Understanding and Motivating Others

Chapter 5: Hierarchy of Needs

The Life Within Call Centers

Look around your call center. What do you see? You should see activity—lots of it. If you don't, something is seriously wrong. Activity is a sign of life in a call center.

A call center, like any other department in a company, is a living, growing thing. It has needs and is constantly changing. It must be nourished and cared for. If handled properly, it will grow. If not, it will certainly die. By understanding the basic needs of your call center, you can ensure its survival and growth.

Survival Mode

At first glance a call center can look a lot like a MASH unit. An army MASH unit is based on speed, volume, and survival. During wars, these units perform many surgeries under very trying circumstances, and they have one goal—to save lives. They can't control how many wounded soldiers they get, what types of injuries they see, or when their patients arrive. When trouble comes, they reacted. In many instances, their goal is only to help the soldiers survive long enough to get them to some other form of care and move on to the next wounded soldier. Their top priority is the survival of as many soldiers as possible.

Call centers in many companies operate similarly. Most call centers usually start out as MASH units. As they grow and mature, they extend beyond the survival mode. Yet many call centers, whether 500 people or 5 people, never seem to get out of survival mode. They get stuck in their basic needs and never progress.

Maslow's Hierarchy of Needs

In 1943, psychologist Abraham Maslow focused on the needs of people in a work environment. His findings became well known as Maslow's Hierarchy of Needs. I'm sure you remember this from your college Psychology 101 class. He listed people's needs as such:

Maslow's: Hierarchy of Needs!

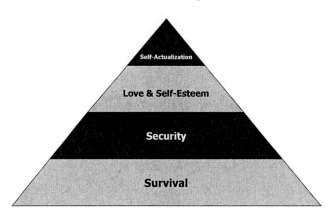

Survival (Physiological Needs)

The most basic needs are survival and physiological needs. These include biological needs such as oxygen, food, water, warmth/coolness, protection from storms, and so forth. These also include safety needs felt by adults during emergencies, periods of disorganization in the social structure (such as widespread rioting). Safety needs are felt more frequently by children, who often display signs of insecurity.

Security (Love, Affection, and Belongingness Needs)

The second level of needs is made up of security needs. These include the needs to escape loneliness and alienation, to give (and receive) love and affection, and the sense of belonging.

Esteem Needs

The next level is esteem needs. These include the need for a stable, firmly based, high level of self-respect and respect from others in order to feel satisfied, self-confident, and valuable. If these needs are not met, the person feels inferior, weak, helpless, and worthless.

Self-Actualization Needs

The highest level of need is called self-actualization needs. Maslow describes self-actualization as an ongoing process. Self-actualizing people are involved in a cause outside their own skins. They are devoted, and they work hard at something very precious to them—usually some calling or vocation.

Michael's Call Center Hierarchy of Needs

Recalling Maslow's Hierarchy of Needs, I thought it would be insightful to take a look at call centers and their hierarchy of needs.

Michael's: Call Center Needs!

People to Answer the Phones

The first and foremost need of a call center is people to answer the phones. This is our survival. Without this security of people, you are dead. Go to any call center and ask any executive or manager what the top fear is, and he or she will say not having enough people show up in the morning! This is why we see so many call centers purchasing staffing and scheduling packages. Without people to fill the seats, you don't even have a fighting chance. Nothing wrecks the survival of a call center manager more than not having enough bodies to cover the business.

37

Another way to look at the concept of "filling the seats" is being focused only on the volume of the calls. In this view, a call center is totally focused on achieving the numbers and making goals that are driven entirely by volume and completion of calls.

> Without people to fill the seats, you don't even have a fighting chance.

Don't lose sight of the role your Voice Response Unit plays in this first area of survival. If your center is built to take 50 percent of the calls through a VRU, the reliability and consistency of that device is critical to your survival. If the VRU goes, you have the same problem as having too few people.

Quality

Performance of these people is our next need. This is where we get our security. Once we have the people in the seats, our security comes from knowing that we are saying and doing the right things. I have seen too many call centers that spend so much time focusing on their basic survival that they never get to quality. They get so mired in trying to fill the seats and meet the volume of calls that nothing else gets done. Worse are those folks who get the people but don't ever implement a quality program to improve their performance. Once we have the people to do the work, we need them to perform the work well for us.

This is why a quality program is so important. There is nothing worse than spending the money to get a job done and having it done poorly, having your customers be dissatisfied or not appreciate your efforts. Too often, we do things for our customers that they don't care about or don't agree with.

It is amazing how small the quality monitoring market is right now. With this type of priority, one would expect more investment in this type of technology.

> There is nothing worse than spending the money to get a job done and having it done poorly.

Since this book is so focused on quality, I did give some thought to putting quality first to really make the point. However, quality really is our security and not our survival. What is important is that you really can't have one without the other. Without a focus on quality in a call center, you will have a miserable experience day in and day out. I promise you that there will be days of misery compounded by frustration and lost customers.

"Jazzed" People

For Maslow it is self-esteem. For the call center it is "jazzed" people. These are folks that are enthusiastic about their jobs and environments. Sadly, many call centers never get to this level. We need our agents to be excited. They won't be excited every day, but you need to have a purposeful process and set of programs to keep them jazzed about working for you. This is clearly one of the key components of world-class call centers.

> We need our agents to be excited, jazzed about their jobs.

Once the top two priorities are in place, this is a very natural next step for a center to make. Too often we put the "jazzed" programs in place without enough focus on the first two priorities together, and we end up with programs that don't jazz anyone and merely serve as an annoyance. If you have ever golfed before and been told to simply enjoy the beauty of the course and water after you hit your seventh ball in the water, you can understand the frustration.

Clear Compensation and Rewards

For Maslow, next is self-actualization. For a call center, it is clear compensation and rewards. That's pretty boring, isn't it? If we have the right people in the seats, we are providing good quality, and our people are excited, we still need to keep them there or get more people to come our way. World-class call centers have figured out how to reward and improve their people. We need to be able to weather the storm and sustain ourselves for the long run. We can't burn out in a call center. It isn't going away. It isn't getting smaller. We must have the ability to sustain our growth and our energy for several years.

Compensation is a key ingredient to a world-class call center. Many have done this very well (Blue Cross/Blue Shield of Alabama for one), yet many have really messed up. I encourage you to benchmark other companies and understand their programs. It would be very beneficial to match up your executives with theirs to get a perspective from all levels. Great compensation and rewards need to be backed by every level of the organization. If not, they fail.

> Compensation is a key ingredient to a world-class call center.

The challenge is that "clear compensation and rewards" still doesn't match up very well to self-actualization. It is too boring. When I think about self-actualization in Maslow's terms, I think of people like Bill Gates, Michael Jordan, Tiger Woods, and Sandra Day O'Connor. My other comparison to self-actualization in a call center would be Yoda! If we could actually have a Yoda in our call center whispering just the right thing to say for our agents, we would be there! Can't you see it in his gravel-sounding voice …"Don't say that, up-sell him on the black belt. … Feel the Force. … You can do it. … You are doing great!" I guess if we can dream about self-actualization, we can dream about Yoda! Maybe the Nuance-type technology, speech recognition that is conversational, will ultimately be the answer to this problem.

Understanding where your call center fits on the Hierarchy of Needs scale can move your organization forward. If you are stuck at the first level, survival, you are still off to a great start toward improvement because you are reading this book. If you can move your organization to level four, self-actualization, you will be benchmarked, win awards and, most importantly, sell and service your customers successfully.

WRAP-UP

- Call centers have a hierarchy of needs. Know which level your call center is operating on and move toward the next one.

- You may be getting the job done but doing it poorly. Quality is one of the basic needs of a call center.

- Continually look for ways to keep your agents jazzed about their work.

- In order to get on top and stay there, you must compensate and reward your agents effectively.

CHAPTER 6: ROSE AND JACK

Lessons From a Movie

Many years ago we did a take-off on the movie *Titanic*. We created a video that dealt with turnover in call centers. We compared it to the turnover of the *Titanic* ship. Hopefully, it was viewed as more tongue in cheek than black humor. We also used the two main characters of the movie, Jack and Rose, as the stars of our video.

For those who didn't see the movie, Rose is a rich debutante traveling first class with her arranged fiancé and mother. Jack is a drifter who won a ticket for the lowest class section of the ship in a card game five minutes before ship departure. Rose is miserable; Jack is ecstatic. Rose meets Jack, who is carefree and fun and shows her the wild side of things. They fall in love; the boat hits an iceberg; lots of people die. You get the picture!

A Stepping Stone

In our video, Jack and Rose were call center agents. Rose was a new agent, and Jack was showing her the ropes. Jack and Rose in the movie represented a couple of very key elements of call centers today.

In *Titanic*, Jack was an aspiring artist who traveled the world. Many people in call centers are aspiring somethings. They are just using this job as a stepping stone until they begin their dream profession. I have yet to meet the call center agent who claimed, "When I was growing up, I wanted to be a call center agent!" There may come a day, hopefully soon, when that happens (maybe an aspiring agent will say he or she wants to be CRM Web chatter!). The reality is that our call centers are filled with actors, film makers, artists, accountants, future CEO's of Fortune 1000 companies, race car drivers, and a myriad of other professionals.

They are usually with us for a very short time, and yet our responsibility and goal is to make them very successful by motivating and training them to provide world-class customer service.

> The reality is that our call centers are filled with
> actors, film makers, artists, accountants, future CEO's
> of Fortune 1000 companies, race car drivers, and a
> myriad of other professionals.

The "Have To's" and the "Want To's"

The second key element of call centers reflected in the movie was
that Rose and Jack entered the boat with two very different
perspectives. We call these the "have to's" and the "want to's." Rose
had to be on the ship. It was the last place she wanted to be. Jack
wanted to be on the ship. It was the only place he wanted to be.

We see this same scenario every day in business, but nowhere is it
more prevalent than in a call center. At the agent level, we see these
two groups of people working in a number of different ways. Some of
the people in the center *have to* work there because that is their ticket
to another part of the organization. They pay their dues and move on
as quickly as possible. These people can be difficult to deal with on a
daily basis because their heart is in working in another area.

Another group of "have to" workers are those who took the jobs just
because they could get them. Call center jobs are well advertised and,
if you are in the right area, easy to get. We all know that the norm is
"get me a warm body ... we will chance the rest." Companies are
riddled with workers in call centers who have worked the "circuit" of
centers in the area—each one with slightly better hourly wages,
benefits, or hours of work.

The final "have to's" are everywhere in our organizations and not
just call centers. Everything they do that requires some effort or
energy makes them miserable. They are a walking "little black rain
cloud." I can easily get aggravated just writing about the "have to's."
They are motivated to be "somewhere else." The reality is that we
want them somewhere else as well. Our success ultimately depends on
getting them somewhere else sooner rather than later.

> The "have to's" and the "want to's" enter their jobs with
> very different perspectives.

Others fit into the "want to" category. Once again, there are
different types. First are the part-time employees, and this is the

perfect job for them. It may meet their schedules, geographical location, or financial needs. Another set of "want to" workers is the group that is motivated by fun and fame. Those in this group love communicating with people, and call center jobs meet their needs. The final group is comprised of those employees who are just built to excel. They love the challenge of their job and want to do it better.

Put the two different motivations of "want to" and "have to" people under the same supervisor, and you have created a complicated situation. Supervisors face the challenge of motivating the agents no matter what category they fall in within the center. Don't forget that supervisors also fit into the want to and have to buckets as well. They get the added pleasure of dealing with the expectations of their executives as well. I have never seen an explanation such as "We had too many "have to's" today to make our numbers!" For the most part, the supervisors are the responsible party for the work output. This requires an understanding of how to motivate people.

Fame or Fun?

For years, in any and every interview I would always ask the same basic question: "What motivates you? Is it fear, fame, fun or fortune?"

Different things motivate different people within the company. Call center personnel are no different. The challenge is the arena in which we are working. They probably aren't driven by fortune. If so, they are in the wrong part of the company. (Author's note: If people are driven to your call center for money, please e-mail me immediately!) Nor are they usually driven by fear. This leaves fame and fun. You can see both of these in the great call centers. They are selling lots of fame and lots of fun. Exciting call centers have a formula for this, and it works for them. Do you have a process and a program for fun and fame in your call center?

> **Movie Quote:**
> **"Cowabunga Dude!"**
> —Teenage Mutant Ninja Turtles [2]
>
> **Personal Comment:** If you work in corporate America, you are probably not having enough fun. I know it, and you know it. I recently read a ridiculous article on CEOs and how proud they were about not getting any sleep. Pretty unimpressive. Get enough sleep, have fun, be pleasantly obnoxious, and enjoy your job. Get jazzed about what you are doing. When in doubt, substitute enthusiasm for intelligence. I have been doing it for years. It works!
>
> **Business Application:** You can't expect your employees to get excited about their jobs, if you are not excited about yours. Make it a priority to create a fun and exciting work atmosphere.

Two Companies That Are Doing It Right

I have had the privilege of seeing many call centers over the years. The best of the best always have the most motivated agents and the most creative supervisors and leaders. Two organizations stand out for me in leadership and creativity. These are Blue Cross Blue Shield of Alabama and IBM Service Organization.

Blue Cross / Blue Shield of Alabama

Tony Carter led the BC/BS of Alabama call center to amazing quality standards by being creative and finding a key to quality improvement. Executives knew the key to their success was a focus on quality. They needed to create a program that would clearly express their priority to their agents. Each week, a representative had an opportunity to earn an extra $100 for meeting quality goals. The program was a success for everyone. The agents had an opportunity to make more money. BC/BS improved quality while also increasing call volume by 25 percent. Read that again—25 percent! Technology vendors in this industry would crawl on their hands and knees across the Sahara in a sandstorm on Christmas Day to get that kind of improvement.

BC/BS of Alabama accomplished this with no massive technology changes, just straightforward focus, vision, and clear compensation. The call center's efforts were recognized each year with an awards dinner for the top performers and an opportunity to meet with senior company executives. The program was a huge success.

IBM Service Organization

At IBM, Olivette Whipple was finding new and unique ways to make sure that her organization operated at a world-class level. IBM has some of the most unique and creative incentive programs in the world. IBM implemented a game called Call Center Bingo. Call Center bingo was the same game of bingo that we all love just played throughout the day while the agents were on the phones.

The game was always played on Mondays. Why Mondays? What is the busiest day of the week in a call center? Monday! What is the day of the week that agents are most likely to be absent? Monday! They played the game throughout the day. It worked better than IBM could have expected. Attendance was better on Mondays. Adherence to the daily schedule for breaks was better on Mondays because people wanted to be in their seats on time so they would not miss any opportunity. Finally, they received a benefit that they hadn't thought of when they planned the game. Accuracy and quality improved tremendously. The reason: people were very focused on their workstation to get the next bingo number and were more attentive to their work duties as well.

Another prize IBM awarded was called Managers Valet. In this game, the best agents of the week had their car parked and picked up by the managers. The larger the parking lot, the more fun the game was. Unfortunately for IBM, the very first week they ran the program the agents start time was 5 A.M.! What a great program! It didn't break the budget, and it motivated the agents to improve their performance.

What motivates Rose, Jack, actors, future CEOs, and accountants? Ask brilliant and creative leaders like Tony Carter and Olivette Whipple!

> ### WRAP-UP
>
> - Call centers are full of two types of people: those who *have* to be there and those who *want* to be there. Work toward motivating both.
> - Find ways to bring fame and fun into your call center.
> - Look at other companies that are doing it right like IBM and Blue Cross/Blue Shield of Alabama. Model some of your programs after them.

Chapter 7: The Call Center Garden

It's the People

In the spring of 2001, I had the privilege of going to Washington, D.C. to get an insider's look at our government at work. I was with a group of about fifty people. We visited the CIA, the White House, and the State Department. We heard from senators, Cabinet members, the Joint Chiefs of Staff, newspaper columnists, and TV personalities. It was an amazing opportunity to get a firsthand look at the beginning of the George W. Bush administration.

Every one of the fifty speakers we heard was there to give us insight into the new administration. Each of them shared with us the same two new changes that President Bush had put in place and communicated. First, he demanded that all meetings be on time. The President wanted to have an on-time administration. He led the way in making sure that meetings started on time and ended on time. Second, no cell phones were allowed in meetings. Every person that spoke to us asked us to turn our cell phones off. It had been only three months since the President had taken office, yet all these different people communicated the same messages from him. Those were the messages he wanted to emphasize to his administration.

Sometimes the message that is remembered most is not the one that you expect. Former President Clinton said a lot of things during his time as President. As I have been around the country I have asked audiences to tell me what was the single most important statement or comment President Clinton made during his eight years in the White House. If you are like the majority, it doesn't take you too long to remember the famous words "I didn't have sex with that woman." Second by the way was "I didn't inhale." You would think that this would be the statement I would remember most also. It wasn't. The statement that stuck in my mind was one he said before he became President, during his presidential campaign. His statement was "It's the economy, stupid!"

I remember that statement because I thought it was brilliant. It was straight to the point, no beating around the bush (no pun intended here!); it was just plain accurate. It makes sense to me because, for a business, especially a call center, the slogan is the same, just the noun is different. In business, the statement is "It's the PEOPLE, stupid."

In a previous chapter, we talked about a call center being alive. The element that gives it life is people. They determine whether the call center will succeed or fail. Because of this, understanding the needs and motivations of people can be the single most important thing a leader does for his or her call center.

No matter how much we automate, transfer to self-support, or re-engineer, we are always going to have the privilege of working with customer service representatives. If you are a manager or agent today in a call center, then I am sure you are relieved to hear this. Every time some new form of automation is added, the benefits are usually substantial. In every instance where we automate or eliminate calls we are always left with a group of more complicated calls. This consistently makes the job of supporting, motivating, and training our call center staff more challenging.

> Understanding the needs and motivations of people can be the single most important thing a supervisor does for his or her call center.

Budding Employees

It all started with a garden. If you don't believe me, then check out Genesis 2:8!

One person who understands the importance of people in a business is Dr. Dick Grote (www.groteconsulting.com). Dr. Grote is a very successful author, speaker, and businessperson. I had the privilege of hearing him speak to a small group of business leaders about their employees. He compared employees in a company to flowers in a garden. His comments and direction on how to look at your employees really made a difference to me. He inspired me to really take a look at the call center and the people in it.

The Garden of Your Call Center

Dandelions	Daisies	Roses
Punish	*Ignore*	*Reward*
Eliminate	Reward	Challenge

Take a moment and begin to picture your call center in a different way. It is really a garden filled with a variety of plants that make up the floral arrangement you call your company. This floral arrangement is made up of three distinct types of plants: Roses, Daisies, and Weeds (Dandelions for political correctness!). These three plants represent the people in your call center or company. Each type has a unique position and contribution to make to your company.

> Your call is really a garden filled with a variety of plants that make up the floral arrangement.

We are going to spend the next three chapters talking about this garden and how you can take advantage of looking at your company in this fashion.

WRAP-UP

- The single most important element of a call center is the people.

- Call centers are made up of three types of people: Roses, Daisies, and Weeds.

- Check out www.groteconsulting.com, and you will learn something!

49

rose[1] (rōz)

1. a. Any of numerous shrubs or vines of the genus *Rosa,* having prickly stems, pinnate leaves, and variously colored, often fragrant flowers.
   b. The flower of any of these plants.

The Cream of the Crop

Our first group of call center employees is our Roses. Roses are our best agents. They are the cream of the crop, the best of the best. We never have enough Roses. We want more. We search for Roses, we try to train new Roses, and we are consistently gazing at their performance, wishing that our entire center were made of them.

The rose flower is a beautiful flower, maybe the most beautiful of all the flowers. Roses are valuable, expensive, and reflect beauty and elegance. If you want to send someone a special gift, you send roses. The White House doesn't have a tulip garden or a daffodil garden; it has a Rose Garden! At the same time, roses are difficult to grow. They require special attention, plenty of care, and just the right conditions to make them blossom and grow. Roses are also prickly. If you don't handle them just right, they will hurt you. The sore from the prick of a rose can last a long time.

Our best employees are just like roses. They are beautiful and inspiring. We treasure their contribution. We are fortunate that they work for us, and they can really make the difference between success and failure. They also require plenty of work and special handling. Sometimes the most talented people we have are a little "prickly."

> Our best employees are just like roses. They are beautiful and inspiring. They also require plenty of work and special handling.

The Boston Red Sox signed former Cleveland Indians outfielder Manny Ramirez for over 15 million dollars a year. He is an excellent hitter and an average fielder. His usual position was right field. The manager felt that Mr. Ramirez would be a better fit for left field at Fenway Park. (It is well known that your right fielder is usually a better outfielder and has a better arm than your left fielder). After trying it for a day, Mr. Ramirez decided he didn't want to play left field and was promptly moved back to right field. It doesn't matter who the Rose is, he or she can often be prickly. Even 15 million dollars a year didn't make the employer feel he could tell the "Rose" what to do.

The reality is that we can only have so many Roses. Statistically, only about 25 percent of your team will ever fit into the Rose group. In any environment, a bell curve reflects the normal distribution of talent throughout your call center. It is virtually impossible to have all Roses in your center. This makes the ones we have even more precious and valuable.

How to Make Your Roses Grow

The Garden of Your Call Center

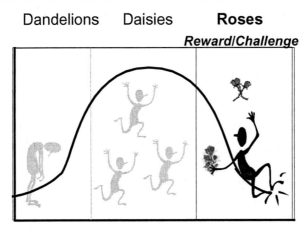

Roses are usually motivated in a call center by being rewarded. We have any number of contests, rewards, and commendations that focus on the Roses in our call center. We know they are good, we tell them they are good, and we reward them for their efforts. However, instead of focusing on rewarding this group, we need to challenge them.

Challenges are what usually wake up Roses in the morning and keep them going throughout the day. Without a challenge, your Roses will become bored and less efficient. The top three reasons for turnover are poor pay, another job within the organization, and boredom. Sometimes boredom is called burnout, but in reality it is the same thing. As I travel the country, I rarely find a call center that has a "challenge" program in place for its Roses.

> Instead of focusing on rewarding this group, we need to challenge them.

We can challenge Roses with new areas of competency, supervisory responsibility, additional education, higher commissions, new technology opportunity, and many other programs. The key is to find out what motivates your Roses and build a program to keep improving their skills and responsibilities.

One of our biggest challenges is that many times our only answer is to reward the Roses by moving them into management positions. In sports, it is usually the poor or average player, not your best player, who becomes a coach. In business we have a tendency to take our best salespeople and make them sales managers. Sometimes it succeeds, but it is always at the expense of pulling our best salespeople from the field. We must be careful that we don't do the same thing to our Roses in our call center.

We talked earlier about a trend toward a customer service being a career instead of just a way to move up to "more important" areas of the company. Today's formula for moving people throughout the organization has been a winning formula. Employees who have dealt with customers and prospects have an invaluable experience in other parts of the company. For the trend to change and help these talented people stay in our call center, we need opportunities and, most importantly, challenges for our Roses to bloom in our call centers.

WRAP-UP

- The best employees are a valuable asset, but they can require special attention.

- Find ways to challenge your Roses rather than simply rewarding them.

- Don't assume Roses always make the best managers. Just because they are talented doesn't mean they will automatically be great managers. You can remove great talent from your group and put in place a lousy manager.

CHAPTER 9: DAISIES

dai·sy (dā′ zē)

1. Any of several plants of the composite family, especially a widely naturalized Eurasian plant *(Chrysanthemum leucanthemum)* having flower heads with a yellow center and white rays. Also called oxeye daisy, white daisy.

2. A low-growing European plant *(Bellis perennis)* having flower heads with pink or white rays. Also called English daisy.

Low-Maintenance Flowers

Our second group of employees is our Daisies. This is by far the largest group of people that we have in our organizations. We all know Daisies. They are beautiful flowers, but they don't require a lot of upkeep. You don't have to fertilize them or give them a lot of care. They simply grow, and they grow beautifully.

This is much like our average employees. They aren't much trouble. They show up and do their jobs. No hassles, no problems, and usually nothing very spectacular. If you really think about it, the majority of employees throughout a company fits into the Daisy category. It is a little like politics. In politics, the people that seem to make all the noise are the people on the far left and far right. Yet, the majority of people are in the middle. Most of the people in the country fit into the ideological middle. What happens to them? Elections focus on the far right and the far left to start and then slowly work their way back to the majority as election day nears.

Our challenge as managers is to avoid the tendency to ignore this group. We don't know what to do with them, so we ignore them. We are too busy fooling around with the Roses and Weeds that we simply ignore the Daisies. In order for us to have a world-class organization, we need to do something different with this group. Instead of ignoring this group, we need to reward them. That's right, I said reward our average performers!

> Instead of ignoring our average performers, we need to reward them.

It happens all the time. There is music and a fanfare of people followed by a long procession of managers. They march through the call center, stop at a cubicle, and make the big announcement, "We would like to recognize Mary Smith, the best average representative of the month! You are SOOOO average! We are very, very proud of you. Mary, I want you to know that there are 198 people here that were better than you were last month! There were also 198 people who were worse performers than you! You were just average. When I think of average people and performance, I think of you. Don't get any better or any worse; just stay right where you are!"

Happens all the time, right? Wrong!

In a call center of 200 people or 20 people, this Daisy group is going to be your majority. We need to find ways to reward and motivate this group.

The Garden of Your Call Center

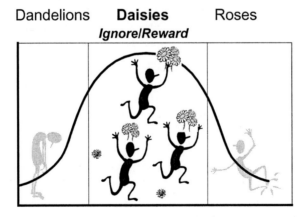

Dandelions   **Daisies**   Roses

Ignore/Reward

The Power of Team Rewards

Rewards are a funny thing. They are meant to motivate, but at times they can do just the opposite. There are many different ways that rewards can accomplish exactly the opposite of what we want. For example, contests and challenges that are too short or not well planned out immediately have a negative impact. The people competing become deflated when they realize they can't win because there is not enough time or the requirements are too difficult. This happens all the time in outside sales. Companies hold a one-month contest with a five-month average sales cycle. Unless you had a deal that was going to close that month, you ignore the contest and feel ripped off.

Another way that rewards can backfire is when one individual or group always wins. Everyone else eventually just stops competing and becomes even less motivated. When this happens, we lose the benefits of the competition itself. Competition by everyone is what makes our center better. If everyone improves, we make massive improvements in productivity.

Some of the most motivating rewards and the ones that get the best results are the team rewards and the awards where there are multiple achievers of the goal. These make the difference and should be one of the first changes that you make as a manager when dealing with the Daisies of your company.

Team rewards have the potential to make a large impact on your call center and, more importantly, on your customers. This is especially true of call centers where small changes from a large group of people can make a significant difference. One of the great benefits of team rewards is that you can have many winners and multiple categories of measurement. Team rewards can include dinners, offsite seminars, plays, gift certificates, days off, lunch with an executive— just to name a few.

> Team rewards have the potential to make a large impact on your call center and, more importantly, on your customers.

Top Rep is an excellent example of an awards program that meets the needs of an organization. Top Rep is a local reward program for the reps and an executive from the firm. It is focused on "edu-tainment," a one-day local program that rewards the agents for achievement at their company. The agents are treated to a day of education, excitement, and personal improvement. Industry leading speakers help them improve both professionally and personally. The executive participating with them helps them to feel special and shows that he or she really does care about the agents' improvement. Finally, the agents feel special and rewarded for a job well done. For more information on Top Rep go to www.tamerpartners.com.

Awards that achieve a certain goal or level allow you to have multiple winners rather than individual winners. For example, achieving a rating of 99 percent on your quality scores for the quarter can have many winners as opposed to picking the top five highest quality scores. Individual rewards can be focused on the area of improvement and targeted for the specific individual.

> Improvement of one person at a time will have substantial benefits for the entire company.

At my old company, we held company or team events on a regular basis. We would hire a bus and take everyone to the movie theater. We went to the mall, had lunch, and let everyone go to the stores for a few hours. We took developers to CompUSA. We had indoor golf tournaments. We had executive car wash days, when we washed all of the employees' cars. We made our factory floor look like a restaurant and served everyone dinner in tuxedoes.

A former major league baseball manager was asked how he dealt with and talked to his star players. His response was somewhat tongue-in-cheek but intuitive. He stated that he didn't have to talk with the stars. They were playing great and already received plenty of attention. He spent his time talking to the average players and the people on the bench. Those were the folks who needed his attention.

I like Daisies. Don't you? If you agree with me, start to reward them and quit ignoring them.

WRAP-UP

- The majority of your employees are not superstars, but they do their job with accuracy and dependability.

- Don't spend so much time with the top performers and the problem employees that you end up ignoring the rest of the group.

- Use team rewards to motivate and inspire average workers to excel.

CHAPTER 10: WEEDS

weed[1] **(w$\bar{e}$d)**

1. A plant considered undesirable, unattractive, or troublesome, especially one growing where it is not wanted, as in a garden.

The Undesirables

Our third group of employees is our Weeds. If I were being politically correct, I would say Dandelions. This is the group that we spend the most time with and that produces the least for us. Our Weeds are our worst employees. These are the employees that we have the most problems with and consistently are the worst performers. You know who they are. To make matters worse, they know who they are! Call centers tell it like it is. We have enough reporting and measurement to know who the good guys and the bad guys are.

> Our Weeds are our worst employees. These are the employees that we have the most problems with and consistently are the worst performers.

Four Types of Weeds

There are many different types of Weeds. They fall into four different categories:

- poor-performing quantity weeds
- quality-challenged weeds
- wrong department weeds
- attitudinal weeds.

We will look at each group separately so you can recognize them and deal with them effectively.

Poor Performing Weeds (Quantity)

This group is slower, less efficient, and massacres our statistics. They are the ones that keep us in the survival mode. Most call center managers are readily aware of these people. We pay a lot of attention to quantity because that is what 85 percent of our reports are focused on. These people are clearly not getting the job done when it comes to quantity. They might be performing poorly in terms of number of calls, talk time, low sales, frequency of putting people on hold, or adherence to schedule. Adherence to schedule can sometimes be the worst area. If they are not in their seats when they are supposed to be, everything tumbles down from there.

Let's look at just one area that can be affected by poor performing weeds:

	Talk Time		Talk Time Improved
100 Roses	230		230
200 Daisies	245		245
100 Weeds	320		290
Average Agent	265		255

In this example, the Weeds have a significantly worse talk time than both the Roses and Daisies. When we make a shift only in the Weeds and not any change in the other two groups, we can make a significant improvement. With a small improvement in the Weeds, the entire contact center is improved. You can see that our ability to have even a small effect on our Weeds can make a difference.

Quality-Challenged Weeds

This group of Weeds simply does not produce quality work. They may consistently meet their numbers and have acceptable talk time, but they lack quality. The biggest problem with these Weeds is that many times you won't see the problems directly in the call center. You will see them in order accuracy, returns, loss of customers, lower up-selling, and the other areas. A quality monitoring program is an excellent way to find these problem people and take action.

Wrong Department Weeds

This group of Weeds is simply misplaced. They are not utilizing their talents to the greatest potential. Perhaps they lack the people skills to be a successful customer service representative but have great technical skills. In the customer service department, they are Weeds. In the IT department, they could be Roses.

Using it as an entry point to a company, many talented people are merely biding time until they can get out of the call center and get into jobs in other departments. This is one of the most predominant strategies for companies: Bring people into the customer service area and then move them up through the company.

This group of people creates a large challenge for a call center manager. These people don't want to be there, but they have to be. As a result, they may have substantial swings in their quality and productivity. They will bounce between Daisies and Weeds and sometimes even become Roses. The problem is that they train well, have all the attributes of a Rose or a Daisy, but can be a Weed merely out of disinterest or lack of attention.

Attitudinal Weeds

This group is usually the smallest but can be the most dangerous. This is the group in which you tend to find the real bad apple or the singular discipline problem that you get from having to hire so many people so fast and at low wages.

These people are mistakes from the beginning. They are a mistake because of everything they do and really nothing that you do. More importantly, these Weeds infect other people.

Getting Rid of Weeds

The Garden of Your Call Center

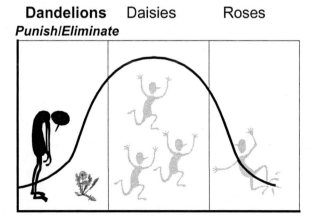

61

Once you realize who your Weeds are, how do you deal with them? Well, generally we tend to punish this group, hoping that they will become Daisies or even Roses. But who are we kidding? Our real goal should be to eliminate them. The challenge is that we have created so many obstacles to this in our corporate environment that it is sometimes virtually impossible to do so.

> Generally, we tend to punish this group, hoping that they will become Daisies or even Roses. Our real goal should be to eliminate them.

We all know what happens when we have a problem employee and we begin the process of elimination. After we recognize the problem, we sit down with the employee and give a "verbal warning." Depending on our HR rules, we may then give them a written warning. About this time we are starting to meet many new friends in HR and possibly even in the legal department. You also may be receiving a "told you so" smirk from HR executive who says, "You asked for warm bodies and I gave you warm bodies!" After a verbal warning, a bunch of written warnings, stacks of papers and opinions on the legal risks, we finally send the employee to another department!

Just kidding. The reality is that the best option we can give our Weeds is an opportunity to work somewhere else, whether it be in another call center (I call this "giving them back to the community") or somewhere else within the company. My former company had many Roses that used to be Weeds in another department.

The other question is how do you prevent Weeds from coming in? Well, that's not always easy. With 30 percent turnover, the pressure to hire can be unrelenting. Even with all this pressure, there is one rule of thumb: Garbage in, garbage out! If you have poor quality, you most likely have poor hiring as well.

> It's imperative to have strong hiring methods and plans in place to keep your call center healthy.

There are numerous companies and technologies available to help you acquire the right talent for your call center. If we are going to have to hire "warm bodies," at least use simulation software to help you have a perspective on where you are starting with your new employees. Software that can help you get some input on the level of talent of the employee you are bringing in will give you a head start on the process. Another answer is to chart and measure your new employees extensively right from the beginning. More monitoring and skill assessment early in the process will allow you to improve their skills or get them out the door quicker.

The reality is that you will always have Weeds. It is inevitable. However, the recognition of Weeds and the role they play in your call center can be the difference between success and failure.

WRAP-UP

- Every call center has Weeds. Knowing how to identify these agents and deal with them can mean the difference between success and failure of the call center.

- Rather than spending time trying to improve poor performers, managers should strive to eliminate them.

- Strong hiring methods and early monitoring programs can prevent Weeds from coming into your call center.

CHAPTER 11: GROWING A BETTER GARDEN

Accept the Bell Curve

The concept of Roses, Daisies, and Weeds in a contact center works. It is an excellent way to look at your call center. If we know this is true and we are inevitably going to have to deal with all three types of people, then what do we do? There is an answer. If you get this one chapter, then you will run a better call center. How well you can improve your results it is totally dependent upon you.

World-class call centers recognize that they can't focus on trying to change the bell curve. You will always have Roses, Daisies, and Weeds. It is inevitable. This seemingly simple recognition helps them to plan their attack on improving their call centers.

Read the paragraph before this again. I know it's simple but just in case you missed it...

Raise the Bar

World-class call centers recognize they can't change the bell curve so each year they move it! That's right, they purposefully, willfully, and through planning, move it. It doesn't matter what you are measuring whether it be cost, quality, productivity, revenue, or anything else.

> World-class call centers recognize they can't change the bell curve so each year they move it! They purposefully, willfully, and through planning, move it.

World Class Call Centers

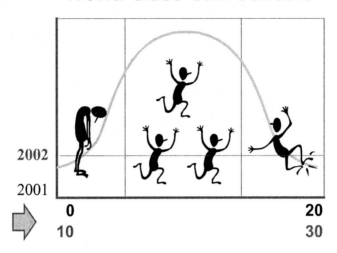

2002

2001

0	20
10	30

The chart above, using a scale of 0 to 20, shows one category of measurement in the year 2001. In the year 2002, the hypothetical call center put plans and change in place to purposely move the bell curve. Nothing else has changed. For example, let's say that you are measuring quality scores on this chart. In 2001 your standard may be 70 to 100. Anything less that a 70 score in quality is unacceptable and the people are not allowed on the phones. In the year 2002, you may increase that to 75 or even 80. This means that you have improved your minimum standards, and as a result, you will have to maintain a better performance. The call center still has Roses, Daisies, and Weeds, but it has better Roses, Daisies, and Weeds this year compared to last year. That is how world-class call centers become world class. Perhaps your call center really has dandelions now!

It's too easy, right? No, it's very hard to do. Yet this is what moves a call center from average or good to world class. These call centers constantly raise the bar.

Many call centers try to focus on areas of the agents' performance that they can really have an impact on. For example, an agent has much more control over adherence, or how close they are to their schedule arrival time and breaks, than they do to the number of calls they actually take. Adherence is totally within their control. Number of calls can be impacted by:

- traffic for the day
- how many people are staffed
- the content of the calls.

Some areas that make excellent targets to raise the bar are:

- adherence
- post-call work-time
- up-selling (if applicable)
- any area of quality.

You'll find that a commitment to raise the bar in any area will have a domino effect. Immediately, you have to change and improve the process you have in place. That is the great thing about raising the bar; it forces you to look differently at your business and challenges.

> Raising the bar forces you to look differently at your business and challenges.

It's always interesting to look at the alternative to raising the bar. What happens if you don't raise the bar each year in some area? What message does that send to your managers and agents? What company doesn't need to improve quality? What would your customers think if they knew you weren't trying to improve? Raising the bar must occur for every area of the call center.

We have a tendency in sales and service to consistently raise the bar for sales goals each year. We are pretty strategic and focused when we raise the bar for the Roses. What we don't spend enough time on is raising the bar throughout the organization, including the Daisies and Weeds. Look at all facets of your business.

- Did you raise the bar this last year?

- Are you planning to raise the bar in the coming year?

- Do you have the support in place to make it happen?

- Are you changing your hiring practice or training to make sure you make the needed improvement?

- Have you targeted those employees who can make improvement?

- Are you ready to eliminate the ones who hold you back?

In the following chapters, you will read about some ways you can improve the overall performance of your call centers by focusing on quality. Through various management techniques and new technologies, you can continually raise the bar and reach your highest goals.

WRAP-UP

- You will always have high, average, and low performances in your call center.

- You can increase the productivity of your call center by raising the standard for everyone according to their placement on the bell curve.

- World-class call centers raise the bar each year.

Section Three

Managing Your Call Center

Sound Bites

Sound bites get such a bad rap today. It seems that wherever you go there is someone taking a shot at a politician or someone else in the news for reducing a very complicated situation into a short sound bite. Sound bites work because they tell something important in a very short amount of time. The fact is that television gets the bad rap about using them, politicians make their living creating them, and the rest of us lament why we can't come up with better ones to describe our daily challenges!

Every business talks about finding just the right comment that we can communicate to a prospect, the person sitting next to us on the airplane, Aunt Bessie, or the perfect interview of a lifetime. This comment is usually described as "The Elevator Pitch." Whatever you say about your company or products needs to be said in the time it takes to ride in an elevator. Elevators today are twice as fast as they were 20 years ago. The average elevator ride is 15 seconds. If you are like most people, you don't even talk in the elevator! However, there are enough plane rides, dinner parties, etc., that we all need a sound bite.

We often joke about sound bites and elevator pitches, yet they say a lot about the strategy of a company and the purpose of the offering that we represent. A call center is no different. It must have a strategy and a purpose.

Driving Forces

In order to develop a strategy and purpose for your call center, you must first understand it. This means spending the time to observe and analyze it. We all know that an executive's time is valuable. The really "Big Kahunas" move very fast, have short meetings, and are constantly late to be somewhere else. This leads me to ask three simple questions:

- Are executives spending enough time in their call centers?
- Can they see the value of it?
- Do they get it?

A customer service organization is twice as hard to run as a sales organization. The challenge is in keeping score. It is very hard to pick a leading indicator to drive the business. We can see the problem right away if we start with the "Big Four"

- cost,
- quality,
- productivity, and
- revenue.

I'm not asking you to decide if any of the four areas are important. We know that they are all important. The question is which one is most important?

> A customer service organization is twice as hard to run as a sales organization.

In sales, it's easy to measure our success in one priority area: revenue. We can set a goal and measure our proximity to it. We are able to see whether we are ahead or behind and by how much. We can make an impact right away. For the other three areas, we can also set goals and measure each category and its impact on revenue. The key is that there is one major goal and responsibility, and that is revenue.

In service, things immediately get more complicated. Revenue is not the clear driving force of the department. As a result, determining the costs and benefits is not so easy. I have asked many executives two questions:

- "How much do you spend on customer service?"
- "Is it too much or too little?"

You'd be surprised how many of them don't know the answer to the first question. The second question is much harder. It is very difficult to make a confident investment in service at the same level that you can make in sales.

Competitive Advantage

What can executives do? How do they make these decisions? Whenever an executive gets to make a clear decision (I define a clear decision as one in which they first get to ask: "What do my customers really want?" v. "Am I going to lose my job this week or month?") the answer ultimately must swing to competitive advantage. Will my customer contact strategy, process, delivery, etc., give us a competitive advantage? If the answer is yes, then decisions get made quickly and measurement becomes a little easier. Some companies don't see service or a call center as a competitive advantage. When this occurs, they are fighting a losing battle that will only end up with lower sales and unhappy customers.

Movie Quote:
"Smalls, you are taking so long my clothes are going out of style."
— Patrick Renna in *The Sandlot* [3]

Personal Comment: People are like sharks; if they aren't moving, they will die. A very smart person once asked me to take a serious look at my life to see if I was just surviving or trying to flourish. Were the decisions I made simply to survive or was I making decisions to flourish? I have tendencies in areas of my life to try and survive only and not flourish. I am sure that you do the same.

Business Application: Nowhere is this idea more prevalent than in a call center. The pace of the business makes change and flexibility a necessity. Companies by nature don't move slowly, people do. Take a serious look at your call center. Have you strategically positioned people, processes, or excuses so that they slow you down? If so, remove them and flourish. You will be amazed by the results.

What is competitive advantage in the 21st century? The answer is quality customer service. It is the area that makes a company stand out and be a leader.

> Some companies don't see service or a call center as a competitive advantage. When this occurs, they are fighting a losing battle that will only end up with lower sales and unhappy customers.

How can executives tell if their call center is strategic to their success and achieving competitive advantage? Simple:

- Where does it show up in your presentations?
- How often do you meet to discuss your center?

- Is one of your "jets" (players, rising stars, well-respected individuals, leaders) running your center?

- Is the leadership of your center a coveted job or a place to hide someone?

- Is it a part of your executive tours? If it is, do you show off the furniture and the view or the actual performance statistics compared to your competition?

- Are you committed to benchmarking? Do you know where you stand?

- When you seek answers to problems, do you look to your center as part of the solution?

- Is your center seen as a strategic place to cut costs or raise revenue?

How many of these questions did you have an answer for right away? Did any of them make you weak in the knees? If none of these areas gave you pause, then either you are running a world-class call center or you just don't care! If there were some questions that you couldn't answer, then you are like most corporations that need improvement.

A Strategy and Purpose

After you have answered the questions listed above and analyzed the role of the call center in your company, you can develop a strategy and purpose for it. This brings us back to the sound bite. The strategy and purpose should be clear enough that you can explain it during an elevator ride.

For the past number of years I have been using the same sound bite for call centers. It is:

> "To provide the highest quality of service for the least amount of cost over the telephone or Web which is profitable to the company and its client."

This is simple and to the point. It tells you why you come to work each day and what the purpose is. Let's break it down.

To Provide the Highest Quality of Service

- What is the highest quality of service?
- Where do we find that number?
- Who decides?

The company has to make that decision. Many times the standard answer you will hear is "The customer does." The customer is one part of the equation, but the company ultimately makes the decision. How does the company decide this? The answer is based on three factors:

- the competition
- what we can afford
- what our customers want.

Each of these factors plays a key role in the equation. There must be a balance.

There are no standards for customer service. The closest thing to a standard has been the mythical equation of "80 percent of our calls answered within 20 seconds." It doesn't fit most industries and is just one of many areas that must be accounted for in a call center. Standards are almost impossible to come by in call centers.

The answer for our level of service is partly in our position with our competition. We are intensely interested in our competition's products, services, and the quality and efficiency of their call centers. When was the last time you faked a call to check out your competition's service or invested in a benchmarking study to compare your call center? It was probably last week, yesterday, or earlier this morning. When comparing yourself to your competition, you must answer these questions:

- Where do we fit in the competitive field?
- Are we the least cost provider?
- Are we the most expensive?
- Do we have the fastest delivery?
- Do we have the highest quality?

These types of questions help us figure out where we are positioned now and where we want to position ourselves in the future. One cautionary note here that we must keep in mind: Our customers don't always look at our competition the same way that we do. One of my former Vice President's wife had separate customer service experiences with a bank, cell phone company, and cable company in

75

the Texas area all on the same day. In each instance, she contacted the customer center to perform a transaction. At the end of the day, she informed her husband that she would be changing banks due to their poor customer service. What is fascinating is that her perception of the bank's level of service was compared to a cellular phone service and a cable company, not another bank. This is critical when deciding where the bar needs to be for your company and the level of service that you provide. Who our company competes with is not necessarily who our customer compares us to each day.

Not knowing where you are going to be positioned makes it impossible even to begin making decisions. I am shocked and usually disappointed when executives can't tell me where they want to be positioned in their call centers. The shock and disappointment comes from the fact that they can talk for hours about their product positioning and service positioning and only minutes on their call center.

We also must be in tune with what we can afford. As call center executives, we must understand this reality. No matter how great our business plan, the commitment of our executive team, or the price of our stock, our resources are limited. We need to know this limit, preferably in terms of cost per call. You would be surprised how many contact centers haven't determined a value or cost per call. They can't answer the question "What is the value of each call?"

The value of each call would be a result of the revenue opportunity minus the cost. Most executives get stuck in a customer service environment, and they can't come up with a revenue value. They get equally hung up on the true cost of the call. At a minimum, the value of your call is at least what you are willing to spend to service the call today. Start with that as your real cost or value of the call. Everything else that you add to this will only increase your awareness of your center.

> If we understand our cost per call, we are in a position to increase or decrease our service levels and understand the financial impact on the organization.

Finally, we need to understand what our customers' priorities are for service. This is almost the same as "what they want," but slightly different. We must understand what is most important to them. Due to competition or lack of funds, we can have only a finite number of service offerings. Let me restate the obvious. We have a finite number of funds—that means that we can only provide a finite number of services. We must pick the right ones. If we understand our customers' priorities, we can better serve them and meet their needs in the order of their importance. The worst thing we can ever do is provide a service or benefit that our customers don't care about and is not important to them.

Perhaps the worst service I ever had in my life was installing a DSL line from Verizon. It took me eight weeks. Maybe that's not surprising to you or even lengthy. It was eight weeks from the original delivery date! I waited on the phone for hours at a time, had over seven different commitment dates for installation after my original, used three different modems, and put up with a host of other problems. Verizon had seven different numbers and services that they "could offer me." Every one of them did something different and "valuable." I didn't need seven numbers—just one that could install my service. (Author's note: Three months after this debacle, I had amazing service from Verizon in their call centers.)

> The worst thing we can ever do is provide a service or benefit that our customers don't care about and is not important to them.

What our competition does, the amount of funds we have, and customers' priorities all work together. Companies spend millions of dollars each year trying to figure out just what their standards should be.

For the Least Amount of Cost

Think about this statement. This is an area where executives and line personnel get into conflict. Executives want a return on their investments. However, the very nature of customer service makes it difficult to put a hard dollar figure on the investment.

Companies want to spend as little as possible—and I mean ALL companies. Even companies that are committed to world-class customer service want to spend as little money as they can to achieve that goal. Not a penny more. How do they decide how little they should spend? Refer back to the top three factors. The concept of spending a little as possible on customer service is sometimes hard for companies to embrace because it just doesn't sound right. We want to have great customer service! We need to spend all sorts of money. I agree. The question is "Can you spend too much money on service?" The answer is, of course, yes!

> Even companies that are committed to world-class customer service want to spend as little money as they can to achieve that goal.

We must recognize that despite the limitations we have on cost, we can still perform extraordinary customer service. Just because we seek to keep our costs in line doesn't mean we can't provide world-class customer service and exceed our customers' expectations. World-class call centers have been run effectively and efficiently for years.

Over the Telephone or Web

We are no longer limited to telephones and the Web. We could add at the kiosk, over the counter, through our salespeople ... you name it! The key here is that each year the CRM areas continue to grow. They take on more tasks, responsibility, and people. Great companies recognize that the perception of the quality of service is tied to all areas. If one fails, they all are affected.

> Who in your company today isn't a customer service or sales agent? Everyone in the company today plays a role in sale and service.

Which Is Profitable to the Company and Its Client

This is where the equation usually breaks down. Every company is set up differently. Some companies consider their service organizations to be "cost centers" and others make them "profit centers." Perhaps you have different names in your organization but you can understand the difference. These are two distinctly different strategies, each with their own strengths and weaknesses.

Companies focused on the cost center in many cases lose their creativity and quite often are not in sync with the changes and goals of the company. Conversely there are very few companies with call centers that view them as cost centers and simply spend "whatever it takes" to get the job done. A company that views its call center, or

CRM center, strictly as a cost center is very focused on keeping costs and ultimately services to an absolute minimum—many times to the detriment of the company's competitive position. This usually happens because company executives don't perceive the call center as being a key component of the firm's competitive products and services. These call centers are usually not run very efficiently, but in rare, rare cases they can be effective.

A company that sees its call center as a profit center has an advantage. A profit center in an organization is a key component of the strategy and purpose of the company. Decisions that are made can have a positive impact on the financial performance of the company. This makes the decisions and actions of the call center an important part of the company. I know it sounds so simple and so obvious, but strangely enough it doesn't always work this way. In tough economic times, profitability and costs are more closely scrutinized.

Herb Kelleher, founder of Southwest Airlines, the most consistently profitable airline in the world, used to say, "We always prepare for the worst of times even in the best of times." If the transaction between our clients and our company are planned in advance and measured to be profitable to the company, then in bad or good times our models work. We build our business to be profitable, and we can control and forecast our level of service.

The second part of this section is the **profitability of the client**. What do they want? In the worst-case scenario, every client is totally different, and you need to market and service each one in a different way. In the best case, they simply want speed, accuracy, and satisfaction meeting or exceeding their standards.

A profitable call to a client is one that is completed quickly, with confidence that the problem or opportunity is solved, and provides satisfaction in a job well done. You can see how important the measurement and pursuit of quality is to this environment. We can be perfect in every area and still not achieve our goals.

In every case, you are back to the individual and his or her perceptions of your business. We often mistakenly restrict the measurement of our results based on only a certain group or sampling. In order to have world-class customer service, we must measure both our clients and our service representatives individually. Without this interaction detail, we won't achieve the profitability for the client.

79

One more point, look for ways that your customers can help you. Sounds strange, doesn't it? However, politicians gain more support and loyalty when someone does something for them than when they do something for someone else. The commitment is stronger, and the relationship is deeper. Just consider how hard it is to remove an incumbent from office.

Author's note: I know a simple way to change the political system in our country. Have national elections on April 15th! Right now, the November elections are just about as far away from tax day as you can get. Incumbent politicians stay in office and by having many parts of their key customer base help them. Do your seek advice or assistance from your customers? Do they participate in your strategy? Is your call center actively involved in having your customers help you in some way? It can be profitable for you and for them.

With all this in mind, what is the strategy and purpose of your call center? What will your sound bite be? Having the right thing to say on an elevator or plane ride won't make or break the success of your call center. However, having a strategy and plan for success can result in a vibrant work environment, achievement of goals, and job security. Those three things will make your elevator rides and plane trips far more pleasant.

WRAP-UP

- You should able to state the strategy and purpose of your call center in the time it takes to ride in an elevator.

- Measuring profitability in a customer service organization is difficult because there is no clear breakdown between costs and revenue brought in.

- In this day and age, quality customer service is the key to having a competitive advantage.

- All strategies should focus on quality, cost, and customer satisfaction. By knowing where you want to be in all these areas, you can develop a clear plan for success.

Chapter 13: Working to Your Pay Scale

Analyze Costs

In the last chapter, we talked about developing a strategy to provide the best quality at the lowest cost. Dr. Jon Anton, of Purdue University and BenchmarkPortal (www.benchmarkportal.com), and his technology group developed a piece of software that I found fascinating. The software is called Meeting Miser. It's designed to help you measure the cost and value of people's time and effort.

Upon entering a meeting, each participant keys in the amount of his or her yearly salary. After everyone arrives, the group uses the software to monitor the cost of the meeting. The cost is measured by calculating the combined hourly rate of everyone at the meeting. It runs like a second clock calculating the cost of the meeting.

If you have some high-powered executives with huge salaries in the meeting, the meter moves very quickly. The idea is to show everyone the actual cost of the meeting. It's brilliant. As soon as someone gets bogged down in the minutia of a subject, he or she can look at the PC and see how much of the company's money is being wasted.

In a call center environment, when you key in the total cost of your center and let the software run, it moves very quickly. The person who is in charge of that call center has an enormous responsibility to get the highest value they can for the investment the company is making in the center.

Providing Value to Your Company

We all know that we inevitably waste money in every area of a company. We put in place process and controls that help us to seek out this waste and try to make it more productive. One of the most strategic wastes of money may be so close to you that you can't even see it. Where do we look? We look right in our own chair. Ouch that hurts! Visions of being called an "empty suit" dance in our head.

We waste money by not working to our pay scale. Working to your pay scale means working at the level, purpose, and responsibility for which you are being compensated. Very often we find that we don't

81

meet the value that has been placed on our jobs. This is especially true the higher one goes in an organization.

> If you often get bogged down in tasks that someone at a lower level can take care of, or make decisions that could be made by others below your level, then you are not working to your pay scale, and you are costing your company valuable time and money. The company can pay other people less money to accomplish those tasks.

Take stock of your daily tasks over the next three days. First, see how many of your tasks are not included in your job description. (Note: If you are an executive and you don't have a job description, then you are important enough to be able to figure out what you should and shouldn't be doing!)

- Which ones are included in someone else's job description?
- Which ones could easily be done by someone else?

Find someone else in the organization to do these tasks. Most people find that leaders are less efficient at their jobs because they're doing other people's jobs for them. If this is the case, remove some of the issues that are keeping you from achieving your goals.

No one should need more work to do than a leader or executive. You should be the person who is available to take on new challenges or tasks. If the hardest working person (task wise) is the leader of the organization, then you have a leadership problem.

If you find an executive who is too busy, you will probably find a person who is working below his or her pay scale. Leaders by nature have a tendency to use the "finger in the dike" plan for most problems. They feel their presence is necessary to keep a focus on the problem areas. The challenge is letting go.

Reassess Your Roses

Many of the areas that you are over-involved in, especially in call centers, are ones that you don't have confidence in another person doing the work. Be very aware that it is virtually never one single person who has all the problems in your group.

> Many of the areas that you are over-involved in,
> especially in call centers, are ones that you don't have
> confidence in another person doing the work.

Most of us focus on the people in our group that we know are weak.
They are the ones we complain about and lament having to take up the
slack for. However, when you take a really hard look at your team, you
will most likely find that your most talented people have problem
areas that you are overlooking.

What happens is that you look past their problems because they are
so talented in other areas. Whose problem is this; your talented people
or you for not recognizing the issue and fixing it? It is harder for you to
see this because they are considered by you to be the Roses or talented
folks in your group.

Take a hard look at your talented people and see if there aren't
areas where you're doing part of their job. You'll have a tendency to
make up the difference, which, in turn, keeps you from working at
your pay scale.

Right now somewhere in your group, division, or company, you
have a very talented person who is a horrible manager. Do yourself,
the company, and that person a favor and move him or her out of
management and into an individual contributor's job. Tell the
employee that he or she can get additional training, but it just isn't
working out at this time. In one quick decision, you can move out
someone who was working below his or her pay scale, move someone
else up, and reduce your involvement in the situation. This is the type
of action you can take to ensure that you and others are working to
your pay scale.

Create a List

> Another way you can work to your pay scale is to keep
> a running list on your desk of "things about your
> business that keep you awake at night."

This list will keep those areas at the forefront of your strategy and
actions. Quality management can help in this area. Almost every area
of a customer contact center can be improved with a quality initiative.

83

Don't get bogged down in the simple process of monitoring calls to focus only on the agents' performance. There is a vast amount of information that is available to solve virtually any problem you may have. This data can be invaluable to your individual success.

Executives often fail to see a contact center as a place that can solve strategic problems in the company. Where else can you find, without lifting as much as a finger, hundreds of thousands of client interactions on every product, service, and offering your company provides? Where else can you find interactions that will be at every different stage of both the sales and service cycle? There is no better place to gather information, implement change, and challenge new ideas than in a contact center.

You can have the same type of list for your personal life as well. Why not use many of the strategies that help you focus on areas of concern and challenges in your personal life?

The next step is to share your list with your managers and supervisors. Allow them to handle some of the problems for you. You can't expect people to read your mind and know what your biggest concerns are—especially if you don't even know what they are. By creating a list of these concerns, you can focus your attention on some of the problems and let other people solve the rest for you.

The same idea holds true for your personal life. By sharing your concerns and challenges with people who love you, you can work together to find simple solution. You would be surprised at the advice you can receive from your spouse, parents, and even your kids if you share your concerns with them.

Movie Quote:
"You want the truth? You can't handle the truth!"
—Jack Nicholson in *A Few Good Men* [4]

Business Application: In customer service and certainly in sales, knowing the truth is the difference between success and failure. You need to surround yourselves with people who will tell you the truth or will find it out for you. Anything less is unacceptable. Make a list of the people you can trust right now in your workplace. If you can't trust them, why are they working for you? If you don't have faith in the people that you work with, you will never succeed. Do you trust your boss? If not, get a new one. It may require you to go to another company, but it will be worth it.

Find Temporary Jobs

We hire temps because they can work in many areas of our company. We see the benefit for year-end peak calling, administrative help, and areas of consulting. If they work so well, why don't we use the same program on a regular basis inside our business? Create temporary jobs for permanent employees to ensure that everyone is working on their pay scale.

One temporary job might be putting someone in charge of cutting costs full-time! We often put our cost-cutting people in accounting. We only bring them out with a suggestion box or during difficult times. Put someone from operations in charge of this area, and you will be surprised at the results. Give that person a title. Vice president of cost cutting has a nice ring to it. Then, judge the employee by how well he or she performs over the course of a year. When one problem is solved, move him or her on to the next one.

> Create temporary jobs for permanent employees to ensure that everyone is working on their pay scale.

Another temporary job is the job to eliminate jobs. Find a talented person and strategically place this person in areas where you think there is an opportunity to reduce or eliminate a task. Give the employee the responsibility to work out of that job. Everyone should know that his or her task is to eliminate that position.

The employee will delegate responsibility to other people in that department or eliminate the tasks altogether. Having a "jet" eliminate his or her job and move on to another one to eliminate is very powerful and very healthy. Executives who work to their pay scale find new resources to spend by eliminating and sometimes creating new jobs and responsibilities that make your business better.

Be the Only Guesser in Your Group

Empowerment is a great thing and a strategy for a call center that we need to employ. If you have a member of your team at any level that is committed to tackling a problem and has put in the time and energy to research and plan the success of his or her idea, go with it.

There is nothing more empowering than implementing "your idea" for your company. If a person doesn't do any of the above and you still have to make a decision, you do the guessing. A CEO or leader should be the only professional guesser in the company. This is especially true in sales and sales strategy. The salesperson is always right until he or she is not prepared, then management gets to "wing it".

> Empowerment is a great thing and a strategy you should employ.

Call centers by their nature are fast moving and inundated with daily crisis. If you want, you can spend each day putting out fires and waiting for the next one to erupt. Each individual call or Web interaction has the ability to negatively impact the rest of your day, week, or month. Strategy and preparation in such a fast moving environment is crucial to success. If your folks understand that they need to be prepared and accountable to make decisions, they will be ready. As the only professional guesser on your team, you will improve planning or be in a position to find new team members who can plan.

Movie Quote:
"I feel the need, the need for speed."
　　　　　　　　　　　　—Tom Cruise in *Top Gun* [5]

Personal Comment: If you are notorious for making slow decisions, practice making quick ones on small issues. It will help you to move faster. There are so many lessons to learn from the Internet. It has made everything and everyone faster. What is amazing is how fast everyone made money and then lost it on Internet-related companies. Though it has benefits, speed also kills. You have to learn to master it, or you will get hurt.

Business Application: Business leaders don't move fast enough. The bigger the company, the slower we move. The best measurement of the speed of your organization is how fast you make decisions. Companies that are slow to make decisions are slow to implement them as well. If you commit to making quick decisions, it will force you to improve your process so you can make good decisions rather than quick bad ones.

Get A Different Perspective

Quite often when I speak, I will stand on a chair or even sit on the floor to get a different perspective of the room. That different perspective is something that most executives and managers seek as they take on the problems that come before them in their daily tasks.

> We spend so much time thinking about problems and challenges, that we are thirsty for other advice and opinions.

For years, I used to pound away on a problem on my own without seeking help. Sometimes I would have spent hours, days, or months thinking and strategizing over some issue, either big or small. I would then take it to my staff for a fresh perspective or different angle and to let them "out think" me. I wasn't playing a game. I really was looking for something fresh and different. Time after time I would find myself totally frustrated as they came up with the same or fewer answers that I had. This was compounded by the fact that it had taken them hours and sometimes days to get to where I was already. However, looking back, they were much smarter than I was because it took me weeks to get where they were in just a couple of hours.

After many frustrating meetings, I made a major change. I began to start my problem-solving sessions with them by first telling my staff what I had learned and contemplated. I told them all my angles and perspectives, all my dead ends and exciting ideas. I gave them every bit of information I had gathered. I asked them to build on what I had already done. They were welcome to correct my assumptions and conclusions, but this gave them a head start. Sometimes working to your pay grade is not being the one who does the final decision-making and analysis. Sometimes we need to be first and do the set up and research and then let our team put the final pieces together.

CEOs and leaders are always looking for something different, something they didn't know before. The very nature of our jobs is to think ahead and lead companies. For that very reason, much time is spent looking at challenges. We gravitate toward a different perspective, view, or idea. The challenge of call centers brings a unique perspective to the daily problems of a business environment. The challenge is that many executives have missed this perspective because they don't work to their pay grade.

There are many ways you can make sure that you and others work to your pay scale. Keeping a focus on your tasks and responsibilities will help you become more efficient and utilize your greatest talents. Then, you can begin to look your boss and, more importantly, your employees in the eye because you are earning your paycheck.

WRAP-UP

- Work to your pay scale by delegating and reassigning tasks that someone on a lower level can handle.

- Keeping a list of concerns can help you stay focused and allow others to solve some problems for you.

- Temporary jobs can encourage employees to grow out of a position and reduce unnecessary tasks.

- Allow others to work to their pay scale by seeking their advice and perspectives.

CHAPTER 14: PROFESSIONAL ENERGY SUCKER

Seagull Management

Many years ago I worked for someone who practiced what we termed "Seagull Management." It was a unique style of management that perhaps many of you have experienced. Our leader always used it after we had a particularly hard day or tough week when we felt like we had really put forth effort but it just hadn't happened for us. As a way of addressing the low morale, our boss would pursue the "Seagull Management" theory. It had four parts to it. He would:

- fly in
- ruffle everyone's feathers
- "pooh" all over everyone
- fly out.

It never failed. We would be down and looking for motivation. He would fly in, work every one into a frenzy, bring us down even more, and then leave. The damage was always worse after he left than before he came. We had less respect for him and the company. Even worse, it always took us twice as long to get back up and going again.

Have you seen any seagull droppings around your office lately? Have you left any seagull droppings for anyone else lately? If so, you have experienced just one of many actions in business today that creates a horribly painful and excruciating sound. This sound saps the energy and life out of all around it. It vibrates through every nook and cranny of your organization, oozing, bleeding, and destroying everything near it. It is the sound of a Professional Energy Sucker.

The Sucking Energy Sound

> Whenever anyone enters my office, I immediately do an "energy test." Is this person bringing positive or negative energy into my office?

Nothing mystical here, it's simply a test to see if this person is going to drain the life right out of me or going to lift me up. A person can deliver bad news in a way that doesn't drain the energy out of you. You can equally deliver good news and still drain the energy out of the room. You know who these people are, right?

There were many days when the same two people would come into my office. One always delivered bad news. However, he always did it in a positive manner. The other would have some good news on one day and bad on another, but he always drained the energy right out of me. I intentionally removed him from my office and eventually removed him from the company.

Take a look at your calendar right now. ... I'm waiting!

I know you have a smile on your face because you can clearly see in your mind the folks who are going to drain the energy out of you. If you can, schedule out the energy suckers, and get them off your appointment list. Don't hang around with them, don't meet with them, and certainly don't give them extra opportunity to drain you. Remove them from your schedule and then your life! When they walk in the door, send them back out until they can keep from sucking the energy out of you.

If you can't keep yourself away from this type of people, your job will be miserable. If you have a problem identifying these people, ask your business partner, secretary, spouse, kids or anyone else in the office who your energy suckers are. I guarantee you they will all come up with the same names.

There are two more people that I want to talk about specifically who are energy drainers. Both are critically important to you. The first one is your boss, and the second one is you. Is your boss this type of person? When you looked at your calendar, was your boss the first person who popped into your mind? More importantly, are you one of these people? Do you suck the energy out of your co-workers, customers, spouse, kids, or parents?

I would love to zero in on your boss first. It would be easy and fun, but let's start at home. I have found that, for the most part, every one of us is an energy drainer. There are just some types of situations in which we find ourselves dragging others down.

My two most challenging areas at my company were people who had no passion for their work and, strangely enough, sales management. I always had an excuse for the first group. The second was a problem that I had to work on. I have always fancied myself to be a pretty good salesperson, so my level of tolerance was pretty low with sales managers. Whenever there was a problem, I felt that the person in question was getting weak and finding excuses. My first reaction was that the sales management employee was setting me up for future failure. What was crazy was that I loved salespeople. They were my very favorite people to be around. I got jazzed just being around them, yet many times I was the one draining energy out of them. I worked very hard to start with a positive attitude every time I met with them.

If you are draining the energy out of your peers, subordinates, spouse, kids, whoever, stop it now! Start focusing on being positive and prepare yourself for the next time you meet.

I was watching my daughter during a cheerleading competition several years ago. Each of the cheerleaders had this excruciating smile on her face. I say excruciating because it almost looked painful. Each would literally contort her face back and forth to make these amazing smiles. They were determined to smile and literally "put on a happy face." What I noticed was that if I stared at one of them, it looked pretty ridiculous. However, if I looked at the whole team, they gave off a positive impression.

Put a smile on your face and make a commitment to be positive and upbeat no matter what the subject. You can do it. It isn't hard; it just takes preparation and practice. We put clothes on each day to make some sort of a statement or position about ourselves, especially when the day or event is important. Do the same thing with your attitude, especially in situations in which you have a tendency to be an energy drainer.

> If you are draining the energy out of your peers, subordinates, spouse, kids, whoever, stop it now!

If I reread the last paragraph, my brilliant advice for not being an energy drainer is to put a smile on your face and make the energy-draining tendency go away. That is the result of being purposeful about your awareness and attitude. The same holds true for working with your boss. If you want to keep your job, move up in your job, or enjoy your job, you must be able to work with your boss. More importantly, the boss must be able to work with you. It is your responsibility to have a positive attitude, even if the boss doesn't. If you are draining the energy out of your boss, changing to a positive attitude may save your job.

If you find that you can't take yourself out of the tailspin of being an energy drainer, I would encourage you to seek counseling and see if you need further help. I have run into many, many people in the work environment who had habitual bouts of depression. Get help now; your career and maybe your very health depends on it.

Company Martyrs

Another type of person I want to address are those who have taken it upon themselves to be the conscience of the company or the ones who have to "tell it like it is." A better term would be the company martyrs. You know who they are.

I know that if you close your eyes you can see them coming from a mile away. These are the folks that have the look of solemn purpose on their faces. They either have bad news, are looking for bad news, or can't wait for someone to stop by with some bad news. They sometimes call themselves the "lightning rod" or the company "mom or dad." For some, it is the pure gossip that gets them going. They want to know the "inside scoop" or have the latest rumor for all to hear. For others, their purpose can actually be pure. They want to tell it like it is or make people see the downside or the risks. They want to help people from making a mistake or let you know who is upset.

> Company martyrs are those people who have taken it upon themselves to be the conscience of the company or the ones who have to "tell it like it is."

Are you this type of person? Stop right now and think about business situations you have had recently with your boss, his or her boss, or anyone else in the management chain. Did you do any of the things listed above? There may be no more important business evaluation you will ever make of yourself. If the negative information didn't start with you, does it have a way of finding you because you are the type of person that will do something with it?

If you are habitually the bearer of bad news, stop now. Have you no concept of history? Do you know what happens to martyrs? They die incredibly painful, awful deaths in rotten, excruciating ways! Don't be a martyr!

If your boss perceives you as one of these types of people, you will eventually have a very painful and excruciating "death" in the company! I know that there are times—often many times—when someone has to deliver the bad news or bring up a difficult and uncomfortable subject. JUST DON'T LET IT ALWAYS BE YOU!

Bring a friend, let an enemy be the lead; just don't create a relationship with your boss in which your meetings are defined as major energy-sucking experiences. It is an unpleasant way to spend your day, and it isn't very good for your career either.

WRAP-UP

- Some people always suck the energy right out of the room. Remove these people from you calendar.

- The company martyr is always the bearer of bad news or the person who tells it like it is. In the end, they usually die horrible deaths.

One Tough Job

Sometime during your career at your company, you put three simple letters together to form one tiny word that has gotten you into this predicament. At the time, you didn't really understand the impact. You had said that word many times before. Little did you know the fire hose of responsibility that came with your utterance. The letters were "y-e-s." Maybe you managed people in another department and you thought this would make a nice change. Perhaps you were a talented customer service representative who toiled for a time in the fray.

You were on the front lines, probably a Rose, a superstar, and the best of the best! Maybe you decided that being "in charge" was the place to be, or perhaps it was simply the money that tempted you.

Whatever the reason, you are now a supervisor, and you have one of the toughest jobs in the call center. Thirty-plus percent turnover, volatile customers, a never-ending supply of new employees, and an ever-growing list of new challenges greet you each day. You are the supervisor of some of the lowest paid and hardest working people at your company.

> You are the supervisor of some of the lowest paid and hardest working people at your company.

Welcome to the world of call centers.

Now that I have painted such a rosy picture of your task, let's look at what you can do each day to make a difference in your company and be a real superstar

It is a privilege to be a leader and a manager. There is nothing more satisfying than taking a team of people and making them better both individually and as a team. Being on the front lines is especially rewarding, but now you get to be a part of the action and, at the same time, be part of the strategy. A frontline leader in a call center is as challenging a supervisor job as there is in business today. Hundreds of thousands of transactions, 240 seconds or less on average to make it successful, unknown problems, and entry-level employees ... you get the message! Wow! What a chance to really make a difference!

Four Strategies

Let's get right to what we can do to help you improve in your job. We will look at four strategies you can use. These are:

1. Keep a running list of your Roses, Daisies, and Weeds.
2. Establish business partnerships with your agents.
3. Remember that your job is to coach, not play.
4. Be a great collector of talent.

Keep a Running List of Your Team Members

It is very important for you to know exactly whom you have on your team and what their strengths and weaknesses are. I have even seen call centers shift people around to make sure they didn't have too many Weeds or Roses. They actually said, "I will trade you two Daisies and one Weed for a Rose and two Weeds!" You are measured by the performance of your team. Make sure that you always know whom you have and where they fit. It will make achieving your goals much easier.

> It is very important for you to know exactly whom you have on your team and what their strengths and weaknesses are.

Having too many of one type of person can make it more difficult to manage your department. As we mentioned earlier, call centers have a mix of Roses, Daisies and Weeds. If you have all Weeds, for example, it is virtually impossible to spend time with each agent and help them improve. Conversely, all Roses sounds nice, but I have yet to see any team in the history of sports that didn't have balance. You need this balance to run a successful call center group. Don't be overly troubled however. The typical 30 percent turnover rate will usually keep your team in a state of flux.

One way to help balance your team is to have your staffing group run your performance based on the quality scores of your team on the phone. This way you can see not only what your productivity level for staffing will be but also your projected quality score.

Establish Business Partnerships

You have the potential to have a conflict-oriented relationship with your agents. They are probably measured more than anyone else in your company. So your reviews and analyses of their abilities and performance can cause conflict. To avoid these conflicts, build an environment that focuses on the positive. You do this by consistently evaluating agents fairly and with detail that they can grab hold of and use to improve their skills. We find many call centers that give away plenty of gifts and prizes, yet have many adversarial relationships. Everyone wants a leader who has his or her best interest in mind. Be one of those leaders.

> To avoid conflicts, build an environment that focuses on the positive.

Make sure that you have clearly communicated what you are looking for in the agents' work. If you communicate your intentions correctly, the agents will perform better.

Call centers are unique. The work product of the agent is performed thousands of times, and every interaction is different because of the status and attitude of the caller. It would be easy to expect nothing of the agent because there is very little that he or she can control. An upset customer might be disturbed because of company procedure. This situation has nothing to do with the agent's performance. It would be simple to blame the company and move on. It is equally easy not to treat the agents as business professionals because they are low-paid or entry-level employees. This is wrong. The key is that every interaction has the potential to be great or really poor.

> We are in the business of producing a team that can get the very best result no matter what the issue or circumstances.

This is truly the definition of the management profession. Getting the very best possible outcome of good and bad situations from our team of people. Treating people with respect and professionalism isn't unique. In a call center, it is essential.

Finally, a professional business relationship means that you understand what your employees' goals and dreams are. One of the many lessons we can learn from both the Gen X and Gen Y call center representatives is that they are extremely interested in their future. You need to understand and have a vested interest in helping them achieve their goals. It doesn't mean that you overlook their problems or pump them up to be more than they are. It does mean that you understand the dreams and goals of your team and you work with them out in the open to achieve them.

Coach, Don't Play

One of the biggest problems supervisors face is doing the job for their agents. Many supervisors have been great agents at one time, and they could easily sit down and do the job for the people they supervise. However, neither you nor the agents benefit from you doing the work. Let them do it, but show them how to do it well.

Great coaches also recognize how to coach all levels—Roses, Daisies and Weeds—to get them to work together and make the group a success. You can't afford to drag along one group or give preferential treatment to another. They must all work toward the same goal.

> One of the biggest problems supervisors face is doing the job for their agents.

I know that one of your jobs will to be "play" in busy times and tight situations. I know that the success of saving a customer may rest in your hands. Still you must coach, not play, if you expect to be a successful supervisor for any length of time and live to tell about it!

It is so important to be in sync with the executives of your company for both your individual career as well as the success of your team. Great leaders keep a list of challenges that keep them awake at night on their desks. Get the list, and make it your goal to help solve the problems! Your challenge will be to make sure that your leader has a list to begin with for you to keep in your strategy. Keep track of your success by seeing how many of the executive's items you can knock off the list. Make it a game and win!

Collect Talent

Another thing you can do is to be a great collector of talent. You can do this by being great at reviews, quality evaluations, and interviewing. There is no better way to be a "jet" or become one than to be a great evaluator and collector of talent. Make it a point to surround yourself with people who have the potential to grow and become Daisies or even Roses. View it like collecting fine art. Each piece should add value to the collection. This will ensure the success of your team and make your job as supervisor much easier.

Every company needs people who inspire others to perform better. That is what made Michael Jordan, Larry Bird, and Magic Johnson so special as basketball players. They made everyone around them better.

Be tough and detailed on your first reviews with your employees. Start them out understanding two very important facts. Number one, you want them to succeed. You are on their team. Second, you are going to be honest and forthright with them about how they can improve.

Having a reputation as someone who hires and develops talent is a great asset. There is no better reputation to have in a company. It is a special talent to hire and collect great people. Anyone and everyone will try to hire you.

Movie Quote:
"You are the best hitter I ever saw."
　　　　—William Brimley in *The Natural* [6]

Personal Comment: You can grow and improve by surrounding yourself with people who inspire you. Choose your friends wisely. Great ones will make you great.

Business Application: Raw talent is so very rare. It is virtually impossible to replace and even harder to find. All great leaders have surrounded themselves with great talent.

Can you pick out great talent? If not, can you hire someone who can? We talk a lot in the book about jets and Roses in your company. Great companies are overloaded with them. Great companies are no different than sports teams. They build a group of talented people and find a way to make them work as a team. Make it a daily obsession to find and keep great talent.

If you pass a bunch of people in your company who give you that "better you than me" look, you know you are a call center supervisor! Be proud; it's a tough job. These strategies can and will work. They can make the difference between having a tough job or turning a tough job into a stepping stone of a great career.

WRAP-UP

- Keeping a list of your employees' strengths and weaknesses can help you balance your team.

- Establishing professional partnerships with your employees will create an environment of mutual respect and teamwork.

- A good supervisor knows when to call the plays and when to join the game.

- Be a great collector of talent. Treat the attraction and retention of great people like the collection of fine art.

A Position of Tremendous Potential

Danger! Beware! Proceed with caution! You have entered one of the fastest growing, rewarding, and most difficult jobs in the world! If you are considering a job in this industry, come on in. The water's a little turbulent, but fine!

If you are already a call center agent, then take heart; you are not alone. Datamonitor reported, "There are 69,500 call centers in the U.S., growing to approximately 78,000 in 2003."

> Three percent of the U.S. working population is currently employed in call centers, for a total of 1.55 million agents.

At a 6.5 percent CAGR (cumulative annual growth rate), the number of agent positions will have grown to 1.979 million by 2002.

Call centers provide great opportunities for entry-level positions into great companies. In addition, they offer tremendous opportunities to arrange your schedule and make effective use of your work time. Due to the extensive number of companies that run call centers, you can work in virtually any type of business or industry, including technology, retail, medical, education, military, government—you name it.

Did you know that at Nintendo every call center agent gets games and toys right at his or her station? Likewise, Talbots has a full store right in the company's call center.

A call center is a wonderful place to get started. Many people work in call centers and also go to school. Part-time work will always be in vogue in a call center. Part-time workers help strong call centers staff appropriately for busy hours and off-peak times. The availability of part-time employment also helps attract many people who cannot put in 40-hour weeks. Being a call center agent can be a rewarding and exciting job. It is also one of the most demanding.

One of the hardest parts of a call center agent's job is the ever-changing nature of the position. Agents in most companies can expect one continued trend: more responsibility. While other jobs inevitably get broken down into smaller tasks, this one tends to keep growing.

> Being a call center agent can be a rewarding and exciting job. It is also one of the most demanding.

The Changing Demands of the Call Center Agent

No job in the entire country has changed faster than that of the call center agent. The requirements and demands of this job continue to rise at an alarming rate. History serves as a reminder of the changes that have taken place.

Emphasis on Speed

Between 15 to 20 years ago, the process was restricted to a telephone and a very simple requirement: "Get 'em on the phone and get 'em off!" That was it. The job was simple and direct. Early call centers were set up for simple transactions. Anonymous callers were routed to a homogenous group of agents. The talk time was kept to the absolute minimum. Service was strictly a cost item. Speed was the key to success in early call centers.

Focus on Quality of Service

After a number of years, a very simple yet dramatic change took place. Competition entered the arena. Having a call center began to give companies a competitive advantage. As a result, companies became more focused on quality of service. The motto changed to "Get 'em on the phone and get 'em off, and while you have them let's ask, 'Is there anything else I can help you with?'"

Today, it sounds kind of simple, but it was a major change in the centers at the time. Asking a question could prompt the customer to take you up on it! This increased talk times, which, in turn, affected calling queues and, ultimately, the cost of servicing a customer.

> After a number of years, a very simple yet dramatic change took place. Companies became more focused on quality of service.

One non-call center example of improving quality of service by trying to fulfill the customer's full needs is the growing number of people who take you all the way to where you need to go rather than just point you to your destination when you ask for help in a store or restaurant.

This used to be one of the really early exclusive service benefits of the Ritz Carlton Hotel. Ritz Carlton would never send you anywhere without taking you. Now you see it in many different areas of business, from restaurants to department stores.

Attempts to Exceed Expectations

The next evolution of the customer service process was a new demand to "exceed their expectations." This concept came from the fact that the call center had finally made the transition from being a part of the service delivery solution to being, in many instances, the *entire* service delivery solution in much of mainstream corporate America.

All of a sudden, we weren't going to get another chance with the client, or maybe this was our first and only chance. Voice response systems and the Internet changed our relationship with our customers. We used to consider it a burden to have to service them and talk with them.

Now, if you're in marketing and have developed and implemented a sophisticated electronic service offering, it's probably a privilege to actually get to talk with them. VRUs don't exceed expectations. Web sites rarely exceed expectations. You, the agent, make the difference.

If you have ever had your expectations exceeded, then you know how valuable it can be. I always have my expectations exceeded at Walt Disney World, Rainforest Café, The Cheesecake Factory restaurant and The Four Seasons Hotel, to give you a small list of companies that include this idea as part of their corporate culture.

> VRUs don't exceed expectations. Web sites rarely exceed expectations. You, the agent, make the difference.

Pursuits to Delight the Customer

Finally, we ratcheted up "exceed their expectations" one more level to "delight them." My best example of the experience of delighting someone is when I go to the movies. If I see a great movie, I know that I am at the "delight" stage when sometime during the movie I look at my watch. This means that I really like the movie, and I don't want it to end.

You intuitively know what it is like to be delighted in a customer service or sales experience. Nordstrom's is known for delighting its customers. It may sound strange, but Starbucks comes pretty close to delighting me when I leave there after having a decaf Mocha frappe with whipped cream and a little chocolate syrup on top!

> A company can delight its customers by really treating them special and making them feel important and valued.

What is fascinating about delighting someone in a call center is that it can be done every day over and over again! You have the opportunity to do that with each and every call. It's not easy, but it can be done!

Requirements To Be Versatile

Other factors are also adding to the increasing responsibilities of agents. Pressure continues to build with the onset of the universal agent. The Web is here. The result is more complicated calls, more competition, more speed, and higher expectations.

The term *universal agent* used to mean that you would take on more tasks. This was sometimes intermixed with a "blended" agent, which meant that sometimes you took inbound calls and sometimes you made outbound calls.

This is further confused by the fact that you could be considered blended if you did sales and service at the same time. Today, a universal agent can also mean someone who takes voice calls, Web chat, and perhaps e-mail as well. Confused?

Simply put from high on up there in the executive offices: "We know you, the call center agent, can do more. We need you to do more, and we expect you to do more! Get the picture?"

Sounds like a lot of other positions in companies today.

Three Strategies

Now that you know what is expected of you, you need to know how you can do these things well. What can you do to improve your performance? You can enhance your skills by following these three strategies:

1. Recognize that you are an entrepreneur; this is your business and your clients. You should treat it as such.

2. Measure yourself, and then find ways to improve and compete.

3. Learn all you can from your contact with the customers.

Be an Entrepreneur

Call center jobs are available everywhere. You have a choice in the type of company you work for. Pick a company that is serious about its center. Choose one that views its customer center as a strategic asset.

Pick a company that has a sound quality program. Ask to see the company's review forms and gather information on how the business does its reviews. Find out everything you can about the type and frequency of education and awards.

Make a decision to be great. Set goals and go after them. Set the right kind. David Boenker of Bana Box, Fort Worth, Texas, states that there are two types of goals; cringe goals and real goals. Cringe goals are the ones that you make and then cringe when you think about them. Real goals are goals you can get excited about and make happen. How many of the goals in your call center are cringe goals? Odds are pretty good if they are cringe goals you aren't reaching them and you never will.

Every time you work with a customer, treat him or her as if you were operating your own business. Make a difference each and every time you take a call or conduct a Web chat.

Taking pride in your individual work will make you stand out and shine. That is what entrepreneurs do in their businesses. They work hard, take pride in their effort, and really make a difference to their customers.

Call center representatives have a unique work product that can be measured independently for its impact on the company. You can view yourself as a business owner and see just how successful you can be.

> **Movie Quote:**
> **"I'll be back!"**
> —Arnold Schwarzenegger in *The Terminator* [7]
>
> **Business Application:** Your customers will be back. The good ones and the bad ones will be back, either to buy more from you or to complain about how you serviced them. We sometimes lose sight of this when we are dealing with problems and multiple interactions.
>
> If we just had one call to take care of, we probably would treat it with quality. Somewhere along the line, we have a tendency to view quantity differently. We become complacent and feel that we inevitably have to lose some of the calls eventually.
>
> Without a serious desire and attitude that they will be back, we will not succeed. I hope our unhappy customers never look or act like the Terminator. Make the customers come back because they want to do business with you again.

Measure Yourself

One of the great parts about working in a call center is that nearly all centers have a myriad of tools to help you improve and measure your performance. Customer centers have extensive reporting tools to see how you are doing. If you are good, you can show everyone! If you are bad, they can show you!

It used to be rare to have the type of job where you could really shine in the company's measurement of you. In a call center, you have a unique opportunity to get a clear and consistent measurement of your progress and performance.

Don't lose the opportunity. No politics, no favorites; just performance. It will rarely happen again in another part of the organization.

Call centers are advanced today with both the currently available and newly developing measurement technology. Take advantage of the reports and reviews. Be a superstar and a Rose. Let everyone see how great you really are.

Industry gurus and futurists are all talking about a new world of white-collar workers who are measured and valued by the information technology of the future. That type of future is occurring right now in call centers and has been for some years. Stand out today, and you will be prepared to stand out and lead tomorrow!

Learn All You Can

Many CEOs started in the call center and customer service area. It is a perfect place to learn many different aspects of the company. You may never get this close to so many customers and clients again in your entire career. What an opportunity!

Listen to what the customers say and don't say. Find out how you can make suggestions to managers and executives and pass on valuable advice from your clients. You may invent the next product, service, or billion-dollar revenue stream for the company! Your ideas may start a new multi-billion dollar product line or save thousands of lives. You have a unique opportunity to make a difference in your career and your knowledge base.

> Be purposeful about your desire to improve and learn. It will pay off for you.

We used to say at our company that we were trying to provide a place to come to work where you could be "better than you have ever been in your life." You have the opportunity and responsibility to excel and really make a difference in your company. This type of opportunity is there for you to conquer in a call center. Be audacious and make an impact!

Never forget, financial trader is one of the most lucrative jobs in the world. There are very few jobs in this world that compare to the millions of dollars in compensation these talented folks receive each year. Hmm... "They spend all day talking on the phone. They rarely leave their seats. They have busy hours and slow periods..." How soon until we have regular call center agents whose value gives them six-figure incomes?

A company's most strategic asset is its people. That's you! A company's biggest cost is also its people. If you're going to be a strategic asset and the company's highest cost, then you make a difference!

WRAP-UP

- Today, call center agents are expected to handle a high volume of calls while offering quality service that delights the customers and exceeds their expectations. It's a difficult job, but it has many great rewards.

- Quality monitoring allows agents to improve their skills and show off their talents.

- Think like an owner. Use the great measurement tools to compete and grow.

- Agents are poised in a fantastic position to learn about the company and advance their careers.

Section Four

Measuring Quality

CHAPTER 17: QUANTITY VERSUS QUALITY

Which Is More Important?

One of the coolest commercials I've ever seen was a Delta Airlines spot in which an agent was talking with a soldier who was in a phone booth, trying to get home for a vacation. After the agent helped him get a flight, he passed the phone to another soldier. The camera then panned back to show a long line of soldiers waiting outside the phone booth. At the end of the day when the supervisor asked the agent how many calls had she taken, she smiled and said, "One!"

A call center is consistently torn over the battle of quantity versus quality. The quagmire deals with the issue of how many versus how well. The conflict between answering the phone calls quickly or taking your time and completing the call correctly has been going on for the past two decades.

> A call center is consistently torn over the battle of quantity versus quality.

In one corner, you have speed, efficiency, and lower expenses. In the other corner, you have quality, customer satisfaction, and improved lifetime value, which should translate into more revenue. Quantity and quality sit uncomfortably in the same ring, yet the pursuit of these goals makes everyone—agent, supervisor, customer, and company—very uncomfortable.

The problem is that we concentrate so much on being efficient (quantity) that we lose the opportunity to be effective (quality). The well-known definition of being efficient is "doing things right." The definition of being effective is "doing the right things."

Until we first decide what the "right things" are, we are wasting our time being efficient. I have seen missed sales opportunities, customer problem sites, business problems, and business failures that resulted from a focus on efficiency without enough attention to effectiveness.

> The problem is that we concentrate so much on being
> efficient (quantity) that we lose the opportunity to be
> effective (quality).

The reality is that most companies focus on productivity. You can
see it on their wall boards, pay scales, and management objectives. If
you don't believe me check your center. See if your wall boards—the
information that you present in real time and "in lights"—has
anything to do with quality.

Check how your "talk meets your walk." I used to give out $100 to
any call center that had quality on their reader boards. In ten years, I
gave out only $400!

If you never measure quality on those signs, you won't achieve your
goals because what you put on those signs shows everyone in your call
center what's important. If you want to "walk the talk," put the quality
scores on your reader wall board displays and watch your call center
quality improve.

Where does that leave quality? Unfortunately, for most companies,
it means that they talk about it a lot more than they do it. Many
executives and managers recognize that they need both quantity and
quality. The challenge is that most of the technology in a call center is
geared towards the "how much" side of the equation.

There's an unending amount of data being produced that will give a
manager all the information he or she needs to determine "how much."
However, instead of spending time measuring "how much," executives
and supervisors should spend their time measuring "how well."

Evaluating Your Commitment to Quality

As I travel the country, I see many call centers struggling with the
balance between quality and productivity. They are searching for the
best way to measure performance and improve. To help them get a
better perspective, I ask the following questions:

- Are you spending too much or too little on customer service
  today?

- What's your cost per call?

- Do you measure quality? If so, how important is it to you?

- What's the single biggest challenge that you have in your call center?

- Do you meet your customers' needs?

- Do you utilize quality management to its fullest potential?

Do you look for ways in which quality management can improve your organization?

Are You Spending Too Much or Too Little?

This is a trick question. There are no set standards in customer service. Most executives don't know the answer to this question. This is why the purchase of customer service technology can be so complicated. Executives don't want to spend any more money than they have to in order to get the job done.

The predominant answer for a call center intuitively is we are not spending enough. We need more people, training, and technology to get the job done. Unless, of course, we are talking to someone who is in the middle of some large CRM project (it's rare to find someone at the "end" of the project) and they may have spent too much with little in terms of results.

Most call centers are not spending correctly in people or technology to help improve their offerings.

> How we spend our money shows what is important to us.

What Is Your Cost Per Call?

You can't answer the question above unless you know the answer to this question first. You would be surprised by how many call center managers don't know the answer to this question. We have discussed the importance of knowing what your cost per call is. It costs you much more money to run your center if you have poor quality. It increases our talk time, number of calls people make, training, and of course revenue and profits.

> It costs you much more money to run your center if you have poor quality.

Our cost per call tells us what we are putting at risk each and every minute we are supporting and servicing our customers.

Do you know your cost per call?

Do You Measure Quality?

Many companies monitor calls for quality but do very little with the information after that point. Many have the program in place but don't understand the strategic benefit it can provide.

> The benefits of quality programs transcend the individual interactions and have a far-reaching impact on marketing, sales, and operations.

We get so busy taking care of our customers and trying to make our center more efficient that we waste valuable information and technology that can benefit us greatly.

What Is Your Single Biggest Challenge?

Everyone is different here. This is where you find out what type of quality areas you need to cover. A well-run quality program will help you meet the biggest challenges that you have in your call center.

You can tell a lot about an organization or team based on their perspective of their biggest challenge. It is a great question to ask. You can't fix a problem or improve your position unless you have a clear understanding of the task ahead. This is no different in a call center. The question is almost as important as the answer itself. An organization that is on purpose about improving their business will know what is their single biggest challenge and the challenge that comes next on the list. This is a company that is moving forward and growing.

> An organization that is on purpose about improving their business will know what is their single biggest challenge and the challenge that comes next on the list.

Do You Meet Your Customers' Needs?

It is critically important to have a detailed understanding of what your customers' needs are. Without this understanding, you have nothing to measure. Many companies have a tendency to fix the

114

problem without ever knowing what the customer's idea of the problem really is.

Quality programs in call centers can help you identify your customers' needs and focus your agents on meeting those needs.

Do You Use Quality Management as a Problem Solver?

At Teknekron Infoswitch, we built a living room in the middle of our company facility. We called it the hunting and fishing room. This room had living room furniture, lamps, coffee tables, and end tables, just like a normal living room. It also had hunting and fishing pictures (we were in Texas!) on two of the walls. The other two walls were floor-to-ceiling marker boards. This room was used for our developers and marketing people to search for new ideas and strategies. We wanted them to be hunting and fishing for new ways to help us meet our clients' needs.

One day we took our best and brightest into the hunting and fishing room and tried to see what problems a call center manager would face and if we could help solve them through quality performance management. In every instance, there was some role that the measurement of quality at the agent, group, location, or enterprise level could solve.

Take a look at the chart below. This is where we need to get to in our analysis and review of our business. We can get from this simple report a very clear first picture of how our team is doing. We see their quality and productivity scores together. How much and How well side by side.

	Quality	Productivity
Donald Duck	9.46	6.80
Mickey Mouse	9.25	9.00
Goofy	9.62	7.00
Pluto	9.20	9.00
Pinocchio	9.35	9.10
Captain Hook	7.65	9.80
Minnie Mouse	9.20	9.00
Total	9.10	8.53

We have a tendency to "hunt and fish" for some-off-the-charts, end-all answer to the challenges we face each day in our call center. If you run a call center today, you have most likely put the required effort in on efficiency/productivity, and you live it every day.

If you are equally committed to improving your quality performance management every day, you will reap additional benefits that extend beyond your productivity/efficiency areas as well. A strong quality program will make you better in all facets of your call center with productivity being at the head of the line in improvement.

WRAP-UP

- All call centers must achieve a balance between quantity and quality. Neither can be sacrificed for the sake of the other.

- A well-run quality program will help you meet the biggest challenges that you have in your call center.

- Call center managers should examine their commitment to quality and then take action to improve it.

CHAPTER 18: A FOCUS ON QUALITY

The Value of Focusing on Quality

When I was younger, I used to leave the light on in my closet each night. My dad would make fun of me and say, "Michael, you're afraid of the dark!" I'd say, "Dad, I'm not afraid of the dark; but I'm really afraid of what lurks in the dark!"

A well-run quality program will "turn on the lights" in your call center and make a substantial difference.

> Quality is the key to a company's competitive advantage. Without it you will not succeed.

Companies must learn to improve the quality of their service without sacrificing quantity.

In the first chapter, we identified quality as one of the three basic elements of call centers. In the previous chapter, we concluded that companies should put more emphasis on measuring quality. But sometimes that's easier said than done.

The performance management industry (where quality monitoring is measured) in call centers is a nice-sized part of the call center business, but it isn't the largest or fastest growing part by any means. It also finds itself far down the line in terms of investment, far behind other capital expenditures. But it shouldn't be. It's the most critical program and measurement that you must achieve to be successful.

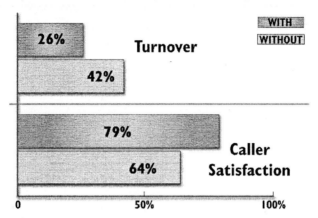

This chart from BenchmarkPortal offers a very telling story. The "with" measurements represent the impact of companies that use quality monitoring technology in their call centers. The "without" are companies that perform these functions manually. You can see the substantial improvement in Turnover and Caller Satisfaction.

Do I have your attention? I hope so.

A quality program in a call center can teach you more about your customers, employees, and business than virtually any expensive, high-powered consulting group ever could. It focuses on the interaction between the company and the client. If we understand our goals and purpose, it's very easy for us to improve our performance. This is why for years we called this industry performance management. That seemed to best describe what we were doing.

Measuring Quality

The measurement of quality in a call center is different from measuring "failures per thousand" in a total quality management program. A great quality measurement program takes the "how well" part of the equation in a call center and takes action!

A quality program must start with the premise of "finding someone doing something right" and then creating a learning experience that will benefit the customers and the employees in the company. It uses the information and experience we gain through monitoring to touch all areas of the company from marketing to manufacturing, sales, development, and, of course, customer service.

> A quality program in a call center can teach you more about your customers, employees, and business than virtually any expensive, high-powered consulting group ever could.

One of the obstacles in measuring quality is that there are hundreds of factors that go into a great performance in a call center. The diversity of these factors makes it difficult to measure and verify the quality in your call center. For example, have you ever asked someone in a call center the simple question "How did you do today?" It seems like a simple question, but for a call center manager it is virtually impossible to answer. Do you mean, "What was my. . .?":

- Average Service Level (ASA)?

- abandon rate?

- agent adherence? (How many agents showed up when they were supposed to be there)

- average talk time?

- up-selling percentage?

- new hires performance?

- training scores?

- network access?

- web activity?

The areas to measure are unending. None of the questions above even address the actual interaction itself. That is ultimately what matters to the customer and the company.

Areas of Measurement

Len Schlesinger, formerly of Harvard University and now of Brown University, states that no team/business—or person for that matter—can really measure more than seven plus or minus two things at a time. That means you can't really measure less than five or more than nine things at a time if you want to get the best results. Seven plus or minus two measurements for your personal life, group, job or company are the right amount of areas to measure. Less than that and your sample is too small; more than that and it is too large to monitor. Great call centers must first figure out what the seven plus or minus two areas they need to measure are and then do them very, very well.

> No person or team should measure more than seven plus or minus two things at a time.

There are so many areas you can measure, depending on your individual call center and company requirements. Here are eight areas that I think are critical to measure:

- Quality (your own scoring)
- Customer Satisfaction (combination of feedback)
- Customer Retention
- Average Delay or Average Speed of Answer
- Turnover
- Adherence (How close to schedule are you?)
- Voice Response Contribution (percent handled through VRU)
- Hiring to Online Time (the time it takes to get an agent up to speed).

Dr. Kay Jackson of Response Design, Ocean City, New Jersey, (www.responsedesign.com) states that we should never measure anything that we aren't going to change. This means that we should measure only the areas in our call centers in which we have intentions to make changes and take action.

Let me give you an example. We monitor the weather. There is nothing we can do about it. On the other hand, we can measure our weight (Sorry!). We can do something about that. Perhaps we don't take action because we don't know how or maybe it's because the change is too painful. At any rate, don't measure performance in the call center if you don't plan to take action to improve it. Is it really that much fun producing all those numbers day after day for no reason?

> We should never measure anything that we aren't
> going to change.

This, for you, may be a very high level view of your call center areas that need to be watched. This list will be different for every call center. You can see that I listed quality as its own area of measurement. I want to show you the impact that quality measurement can have on another area of measurement in the call center. Let's look at number eight, which is Hiring to Online Time.

If you look at the chart below, you can see the impact of getting an agent up to speed in a timely fashion. This chart assumes a burdened rate of $25,000 per year for a representative.

Representative Cost Per Call

Month	(1-2)	(3-4-5)	(6-8)	(9+)
Talk Time	320	300	270	245
Calls Per Day	65	69	77	85
*Cost Per Call	$0.85	$0.81	$0.72	$0.65

Look at the difference between a beginning agent and one with nine months of experience. You can see that the talk time is significantly different (320 seconds vis-a-vis 245 seconds). This impacts both the calls per day and the cost per call. The difference in cost of $0.20 per call is substantially significant when you multiply that times the number of agents and calls a center will handle over the course of a year.

The single biggest contributor to cutting the cost is quality measurement. This table reflects the very real ramp-up time of a new employee. With an average turnover rate of 30 percent, new employees are the norm in our centers. We improve the ramp-up time of new employees by monitoring them more often. This gives us the opportunity to look at many different types of calls to see how they have grasped the different areas that they have been trained in. We let the representative listen to their mistakes and victories to reinforce their training. How do you reduce talk time? We use the quality technology and process to improve the ramp-up time of an agent.

Any investment we can make to speed up the training time can have amazing effects on our business. Imagine if the above example is a revenue opportunity. Think of the impact of twenty more sales calls per day per person. You pick the increase in sales and profits to the bottom line of the company. You should also note that this chart merely takes a Weed to a Daisy. The benefits of moving to a Rose are even more substantial.

We just looked at one area of the eight that I used in our example above. Every area can benefit from quality measurement and management. Later I will show you a chart that emphasizes the benefits even more.

Benchmarking

There are many different areas that can be measured. The next time you go to another call center, ask the managers and staff what they measure. Look closely for their key indicators for their business.

Benchmarking fascinates us as it does people in most other industries. We want to see how the other company is doing it. We want to find the secret to the problem, take advantage of other companies' experiences, and use that data to improve ourselves. Virtually every time call center managers visit another call center to benchmark and "check them out," they walk away with the same feelings. What they see is a company that does some number (usually one to three) of their seven plus or minus two areas very well. What the visiting company invariably walks away with is "ABC corporation really does this area X well. I was impressed, and we should learn from our visit here. BUT did you see this area or that area? We are much better here, and we do this substantially better."

Get your boss or your team together and go benchmark someone else who has a world-class call center. In Chapter 23 we have a list of call centers that are world class.

I promise you that when you go you will be amazed first at how professional and on purpose these companies are about achieving their goals. You will also see that there are many areas in which you already meet and potentially exceed some of the best call centers in the world.

It is really important that you set out the areas in which you want to be successful in your call center. Without that road map, you meander in and out of delivering to your customers what they need. In the long run, your flashes of brilliance will be overcome by your lack of attention to the very details necessary for you to compete and win.

> Benchmarking fascinates us as it does people in most other industries. We want to see how the other company is doing it.

A benchmark tour can either be anecdotal or it can really make a difference. It depends how prepared you are before you arrive. See if you can pick out what areas the center you visit has focused on.

Is anyone benchmarking your call center? Have you won an award for your center? (Author's note: You should apply to win an award for your customer service environment. The application alone will drive you to have a better call center. Technology vendors usually will work with you to fill out an application. They get to bask in the glow of your success.) Yes. Congratulations and now go win another one! No? Make sure you have your seven plus or minus two areas to measure and do one or two of them better than anyone else in the world. Do this and the benchmark tours will be a part of your weekly agenda.

WRAP-UP

- The measurement and improvement of quality in the call center will impact all areas of a company.

- Measuring quality can be difficult because so many factors contribute to great performance.

- To achieve quality, focus on a few specific areas, measure these areas carefully, and perform them better than anyone else.

How Quality Affects the Call Center

One of the challenges of a call center is that there are so many numbers! We are overloaded with numbers to measure and improve. We can seek out any quantity we choose of statistics, ratios, leading indicators, market data, trends, etc.

Don't get me wrong. This is really important and an incredible asset to creating a world-class call center. The harsh reality is that despite this plethora of numbers and statistics, we can never lose sight of the relationships in our center and their impact on our performance.

After all, all these numbers are based on the people in the call center and their interactions with each other.

> Understanding these key relationships and how they are affected by quality measurement can have an enormous impact on your company.

Key Interactions

The quality measurement of the interactions of our people can substantially affect our key relationships. We can use quality to make them better. These relationships are:

1. Agent to Customer
2. Agent to Supervisor
3. Executive to Client.

Agent to Customer

The first relationship that really counts is between your front line employee and your customer. It is amazing how little appreciation other areas of the company have about the value of this interaction. Quality monitoring can have a significant effect on this relationship in many ways. It allows us to see firsthand what really happened in the interaction.

125

As a company, our ability to measure the work product of our agents can often be restricted by a lack of the technology. Live monitoring, while effective, is burdensome and inaccurate. The use of technology allows the representatives to listen to their own work.

> One of the major benefits of quality measurement should be that the agent can review his or her own work.

This is extremely important in improving performance. Monitoring technology enables the agent the same access to his or her performance data as the supervisor.

This means that the agent is empowered to identify his or her own areas that need improvement. In order to be successful in a call center, we need to have the agents want to be as successful with our clients as the company does. Their job is to exceed the expectations of the clients. By giving them the tools necessary to exceed expectations, we can make this happen.

Quality measurement allows the representative to take the data from the supervisor, other agents, and their own review and find new ways that they can improve. If you watch professional sports, you will always find management and the players making adjustments and improvements in their work. The best results come when the players or agents have been given the resources to help themselves.

We are all tuned in to the same radio station, WIIFM. This stands for "What's in it for me?" For example, would you rather have your boss do your year-end review or would you rather do it yourself? Which one of you will remember the most about your performance? Who will remember the most good things and bad things?

Each one of us individually will remember more about ourselves than we ever will about someone else. This is why access to our performance data can positively impact the agent-to-customer relationship. An empowered and frequently monitored agent will perform better every single time, in every single circumstance.

When agents have the ability to review their own work, they will find the problems and the successes.

Many call centers talk a great game about empowering their agents, yet they don't use the agents themselves as a tool to improve their call center and quality process. Letting the agents play a key role in quality measurement will improve the interaction with the client. The result is better sales and relationships.

Agent to Supervisor

The second relationship that quality monitoring positively affects is the relationship between the agent and supervisor. Monitoring by its very nature has the opportunity to create conflict. Even well-meaning supervisors may feel as if they are invading the privacy of their representatives. We have always been taught from the time we were small that we were invading the privacy of the caller when we listened in on someone else's call.

Many supervisors hate to give the yearly or semi-annual reviews to their employees. They don't like the potential for conflict. They find the conversation and review very uncomfortable, or worse, they avoid conflict by not dealing with the real issues. This is by far the worst possible outcome. We could all buy a small cottage by our favorite lake if we had a dollar for each time a manager didn't deal with a real issue. The problem is that when this occurs neither party is served.

A well-run monitoring program removes the doubt and uncertainty from the transaction. Both parties have the actual interaction to examine and the mechanisms in place to be confident in their reviews. There is nothing more empowering than to see and hear the real interaction they are reviewing. This trust is so important. It builds teamwork and a more positive work environment.

When the agent and the supervisor get together, both parties are prepared to discuss the agent's performance. Over and over again we hear that a representative will pick out their mistakes almost immediately. This takes away a large part of the conflict and, in many instances, gives the supervisor the opportunity to focus on the positive parts of the interaction.

> When agents have the ability to review their own work, they will find the problems and the successes.

Another benefit for the supervisor-agent relationship is that a call center can use quality measurement to get to the root of a problem. If you find that there are a number of agents that have a quality problem

127

with a certain type of offering within the company, the answer may very well be the training they received.

Great monitoring software will allow you to measure who actually taught the agents, and you can measure quality performance of the trainers as well. What confidence the supervisors and agents have when they know that the root cause of the problems can be discovered!

Executive to Client

I have left the most powerful relationship change for last. This is the relationship between the executive and the client. If you are a supervisor or member of a call center reading this, make sure your executives read this next part.

Have you ever seen your child display a talent or behavior for the first time that was so positive it almost knocked you over? I'm talking about some talent, characteristic, or action that you knew would make the youngster better able to handle the challenges and obstacles of life. You probably realized that the talent had been there all the time; you just had never noticed it before.

A call center, no matter how large or small, can display the very same thing to an executive. It is this precious resource, gem, or opportunity that they never really understood or didn't take the time to get to know.

It is enjoyable to watch when an executive finally sees the power and potential of a call center. Where else can you go any time of day or night and see the interaction that occurs between your customers and your company?

> It is enjoyable to watch when an executive finally sees the power and potential of a call center.

The problem is that executives are so far removed from this interaction that they fail to realize all they can learn from it. Here is what probably happens in your company: Once a month, once a quarter, or worse, once a year, the executives visit the call center. (If I could pump in "Pomp and Circumstance" music right now, I would.) They come down from their executive offices to much fanfare and excitement. Maybe they sit down and listen to a call. Some may stay for an hour or two, and some may actually take a call or two to really "stay in touch." Wow! After this exercise, they leave and reschedule another visit for some other month or year.

The reality is that they have the opportunity to be in touch with their customers at any time, any day of the week. REAL executives listen, watch, and participate in customer calls all the time. They listen in their cars, office, hotels, and homes to important interactions that occur in their company.

How can they do this? Monitoring technology allows them to listen from anywhere just like voice mail. Key interactions that you want them to understand can be at their fingertips. From their desktop, they can see the entire transaction both voice and the actual screens of the representative taking the call. It is as if they were right there looking over the shoulder of the representative. You can't pay enough money for that kind of market research. Thousands and thousands of interactions, chock full of information to help them run their business better, are just sitting there waiting for the executives to take notice. Getting your executives this information in an easy-to-use, timely, and non-invasive way can change the fortune of your business overnight.

> REAL executives listen, watch, and participate in customer calls all the time.

Changing important relationships that matter is the benefit of automation and quality monitoring. Each relationship by itself can transform your area within the company or the entire company itself. Combined, these three business relationships can vault an organization into the league of world-class companies. If you haven't taken the step, don't just step, plunge! If you have, are you getting out of it all that you can?

WRAP-UP

- Quality measurement can substantially affect the key relationships within a company.

- One of the most important benefits of quality measurement is that it allows the agent to review his or her own work.

- If done correctly, a quality monitoring program can reduce conflicts between the agent and the supervisor.

- Executives should measure quality firsthand to gain a better understanding of their call center and its value.

CHAPTER 20: CALL MONITORING

Reviews: A Potential for Conflict

For some reason we seem to be built for conflict. Maybe it started when we were babies. When we didn't get what we wanted or needed, we cried. The less we got or the longer it took, the louder and more emphatic we became. We created a scene and voiced our disapproval as loud as we could. Wouldn't it be great today if we could throw a temper tantrum every time a prospect said no to us or a customer complained? Just throw a fit and get our way!

For years, the measurement of call center agents has produced conflict for our customer service and sales representatives. I have yet to see anyone throw a hissy fit or crying tantrum, but we do have challenges. For years agents have created a work product that call center leaders have tried valiantly—and sometimes in vain—to measure and improve. This measurement has resulted in conflict. Call center agents have consistently complained about how they are measured.

> For years agents have produced a work product that call center leaders have tried valiantly to measure and improve.

As we discussed in the last chapter, quality measurement can produce adversarial relationships between the supervisors/quality managers and the agents that can inhibit a call center from achieving its goals. It is hard enough just to meet the changing rules, new challenges, and fluctuating standards that are part of everyday life. What a call center doesn't need is conflict and distrust in the one area that can really help: quality measurement.

Three Common Complaints About Measurement

The three major complaints from agents today regarding performance monitoring are the same three that we have had for the past twenty years. The difference is that today technology can help to eliminate these complaints and, at the same time, help the relationship of the reviewer and the agent.

The three complaints are:

- "I didn't say that."
- "You caught me on a bad day."
- "Jane/Joe (the supervisor/quality person) is a hard grader."

"I Didn't Say That"

During a review, some agents will emphatically deny the comments and actions that they are being reviewed for. This could signal one of two situations. Either the agent has forgotten what was said or he or she is simply refusing to "remember." Companies that have invested in recording technology have a tremendous advantage. They actually have a recording of the monitored call to play back for the agent. There is no controversy, no question, or at the very least, something to argue about!

What is fascinating is just how important this really is to a call center. We find many organizations just talking about quality and some *really* taking steps to improve. The problem is that if a call center doesn't create a mechanism for everyone to participate, it won't accomplish its goals.

Why have four executives and perhaps 20 managers focused on quality with 400 agents merely participating in the plan? Instead, why not provide access to everyone in the call center and get 424 (4+20+400) people all moving in the same direction having access to the quality information? Many companies today allow their agents to listen to their calls before they sit down for their reviews.

Let's make sure we define *listen* in terms of technology. Today, you can record the calls, but you can also record the screen the agent is working on as well. This means the agents can also see what they typed into their computer synchronized with the conversation. Wow! They can get a full view of exactly what happened. In our new Web world, the communications performed by e-mail and Web chat can benefit from the same review as the phone conversation. Depending on your investment in technology, the term *listen* can be just voice or the screens as well. In addition, many companies allow the agents to listen to other people's calls and see how they are doing.

Supervisors spend hours calibrating calls to make sure they are all on the same page. Why not give the agents a leg up and give them access to their own calls so they can calibrate calls themselves? Enabling the agent to have access to the actual interactions themselves is one of the quality initiatives that can be implemented the most quickly. It's very simple: show the worker his or her product and help them make it better.

Agent Monitoring/Coaching Results

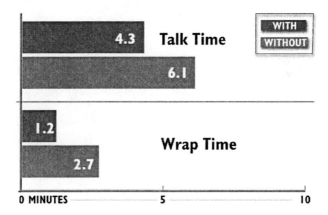

This chart from BenchmarkPortal Inc. shows the impact of quality monitoring technology on two key components of the call—talk time and wrap time. The incredible performance difference speaks volumes about the impact that quality monitoring technology can have on your call center.

> Many companies today allow their agents to listen to their calls before they sit down for their reviews.

For those who have not invested in some sort of recording technology, the challenge is tougher. You are restricted to having your sessions with your agents soon after the actual calls so everyone can remember the interaction. The problem lies in timing. We want to measure our agents in all types of environments throughout the month, including peak hours. However, this means pulling the agent off the phone during these hours to review his or her performance. Even a simple recorder from Radio Shack can help ease this problem.

You can record the calls and then hold the review session at a time convenient for everyone.

There are many success stories of agents who heard themselves on the phone and recognized for the very first time how they sounded, what they said, and what image they projected to their customers.

One travel industry call center agent attended weekly meetings with the supervisor and the team. The supervisor would consistently caution the agents against murmuring while waiting for a screen or additional information. This agent also used to encourage all the others to not do this. When the call center installed recording technology and allowed her to listen to her calls, this is what she heard during a silent period: "Come on, baby, talk to me, bring me my sweet information, tell me, tell me what I need to know..." She was mortified but forever convinced that she also needed to make changes like the others.

Another agent vehemently argued that he was not abrasive to customers. Upon hearing what seemed like a very angry agent talking to a customer his response was "That's me? I really am obnoxious; I can't believe I sound so angry!" Listening to calls and hearing how you sound is extremely effective and corrective for the agents.

There is an unending supply of stories about poorly performing agents who were on their way out of the company. After hearing themselves on the phone, they made substantial improvement and in many cases became Roses.

"You Caught Me On a Bad Day"

The next biggest complaint involves the timing of the review. The agent in question usually says "I am the best rep you have between 2:00 and 2:15 on Thursdays. You just never monitor me during that time." Sure.

This is probably the single biggest risk and change that has occurred in quality monitoring over the last five years. The original problem was that an agent was monitored between five and twelve times a month using some sort of live monitoring or taping. Because the monitoring process was so intrusive, all of these calls were usually taken during one hour or day. The supervisor achieved the goal but didn't affect any sort of random collection of data. What value is there in picking up only seven or ten calls when they are all on the same day and in the same hour? Early monitoring technology was designed to work in conjunction with forecasting and scheduling packages to record calls randomly throughout the month.

There are many monitoring systems that purport to record random calls but, in fact, are simply clumping calls and getting them all at once. Check your monitoring systems.

> It's imperative that we are able to get a sampling of calls or transactions throughout the course of the month.

The more random the calls, the more representative of your agents' true performance the calls will be. With the advent of smarter recording technology, many companies are starting to focus on specific types of calls and situations to record. This is an excellent and valuable practice. However, make sure that you are still using random recording for quality to ensure that you get a sample of different types of situations and a clear perspective on the agent's performance.

Remember that leading call centers monitor between 5 and 15 calls per agent per month at various times of the week and day. This total does not take into account other activities such as e-mail, Web chat, and other types of transactions.

One call center in Canada took it one step further and enabled its agents to listen to all of their recorded calls first. They then picked out the calls that they wanted to be monitored and threw the rest away. Sound risky? Quality improved dramatically and customer complaints went down as well in the call center.

"I Wasn't Graded Fairly"

Finally, the most looming issue is the fairness of the supervisor or quality manager who grades the session. This issue is usually one of calibration and not of any animosity or ongoing desire to "grade more strictly."

Calibration means that the supervisors, managers, and sometimes even the agents get together and listen to calls. They evaluate them and then compare the evaluations to make sure that everyone is in agreement or near agreement about the quality score of the call. This ensures that the scores are valid and representative of what the company and center is trying to accomplish.

Great call centers have implemented programs for calibration either locally or spread out throughout the enterprises. Calibration is critical to fairness and results that have value.

> If you don't have a strong calibration program in place, you will not have strong quality in your call center.

In addition to calibration, you can also address this complaint by "monitoring the monitor." Automation provides the opportunity for the company to monitor the monitor. This gives the company the confidence that it is protected as well. With a clear view of the agents' performance, everyone works from the same perspective.

By monitoring the monitor, we are able to see through any lack of calibration and most important discrimination. Nothing breeds more confidence than to be able to show that a supervisor has treated everyone fairly. You must be able to measure the performance of your monitors (supervisors or quality assurance representatives). Do you regularly measure the scores and compare the supervisors to each other? You can measure by question, group, and agent representative.

Some companies offer incentives to the supervisors for high quality scores for their groups. This can be a great idea and a powerful tool for success. The challenge is that these same companies allow the supervisors to do the quality scoring for their own people. This means everyone scores very high. The company shows reports with high scores, and the agents and supervisors get their rewards, yet the company loses clients! It's critical that, if you pay for performance in the quality area, you have checks and balances in place for the people who score the monitoring performance.

Providing Feedback

We need one more piece here to be complete. Ronald Reagan taught the political world plenty about the importance of presentation. He recognized the importance of communicating a message of any kind in a positive and self-assured way. He knew that the way the message was delivered could be as important as the message itself. His communication style exuded trust. This art is not lost on the quality performance relationship.

Great scores or scores that need improvement when presented in a professional and consistent manner can and will make a difference. As

136

we mentioned previously, this business needs to be about finding someone doing something right. If that is the intention and the culture, you will run a much more vibrant and exciting center.

> Great scores or scores that need improvement when presented in a professional and consistent manner can and will make a difference.

Make sure that you have a detailed and positive plan for providing feedback to your agents. This sounds simple enough. However, you would be surprised how many companies run great programs but blow it when they conduct the reviews.

Recognizing agents' top three complaints is a simple first step to improving your call center. The second and more important step is doing something about it!

WRAP-UP

- Knowing agents' three common complaints about reviews can help you anticipate problems, establish a policy of fairness, and prevent conflicts.

- Recording technology enables agents to listen to their own calls and provides supervisors a more representative sample of the agent's work.

- Direct involvement in the review process empowers agents to identify and improve their skills on their own.

CHAPTER 21: REPORTS

The Purpose of Reports

You have monitored and measured, examined and analyzed, but what next? How do you take your findings and make some sense out of them?

If you're like everyone else, you put them in a report. Reports are either the bane of our existence or the fuel that drives the engine of our call centers. The reality is that we can't live with them and we can't live without them.

> Reports provide us with the valuable opportunity to analyze our results and identify our strengths and weaknesses.

After all, isn't that the whole purpose of measurement?

The Shortcomings of Reports

Despite its lofty purpose, reporting usually falls short of our expectations and needs. Organizations have usually already dug themselves a deep hole when it comes to reporting. Take a look right now at the reports that you use to measure your business. Are they as useful as they need to be?

First, look at the size of the package. How many pages is the daily, weekly, or monthly report? Is the package huge? I have seen packages that have over 40 pages of reports. No one actually looks at them. They just send them out each month.

Second, how many pages of the report do you actually look over each time? Many companies have ended up with a compilation of reports. Everyone has his or her own report, and everyone else gets a copy of it—whether they need it or not. In some rare instances, they still pass around reports that were for people who are no longer in the company! In reality, most people actually use only a small number of the reports they receive.

Third, look at the reports that are most important to you. Is there information in them that you don't need or don't want? I have found that reports have a tendency to expand over time. Rarely do they shrink. Why not have a report that tells you exactly what you need to know and nothing else?

> In reality, most people actually use only a small number of the reports they receive.

Fourth, is the information timely enough for you to do anything about it? If you make most of your decisions in the first week of the month and your reporting comes on the second week, how useful is it?

For years we worked with management information reporting. The Teknekron Infoswitch ACD had the best reporting in the marketplace for the majority of the 1980s. We coined the phrase "If you can't measure it, you can't manage it." As a matter of fact, there are still some of those switches installed, and they probably still have a better management information package than some ACD's today.

Re-examine your reports and find ways to make them more useful. Focus on clarifying the information you need and getting rid of everything else. Remember, unnecessary information is a waste of time—and trees.

Interactive Detail Versus Average Data

Some call centers are operated strictly on averages. However, world-class call centers recognize that this is a certain recipe for failure. Managers and supervisors must be able to get to the interaction detail that makes up the averages. "Average data" is fine as long as you have the interaction data to back up the averages.

> Managers and supervisors must be able to get to the interaction detail that makes up the averages.

	TALK TIME										
Call:	1	2	3	4	5	6	7	8	9	10	AVERAGE
Agent X	298	302	298	298	302	302	298	302	302	298	300
Agent Y	598	2	2	2	598	2	598	2	598	598	300

Let me give you an example. Agent X takes five calls, each lasting 4 minutes and 58 seconds. He also takes five calls that each last 5 minutes and 2 seconds. The average call length for these 10 calls is exactly 5 minutes. Agent Y takes five calls that each last 9 minutes and 58 seconds. He also takes five calls that are dumped at 2 seconds each. The average call length for these ten calls is also exactly five minutes. These two agents have the same statistics, yet one is getting a raise and the other is being given back to the community!

We need the interaction data to find out what really happened. To put it another way, if I have one leg in hot scalding water and the other leg in freezing cold water, on average the temperature is fine. I won't be having any more kids, but the temperature is fine!

This recipe for disaster is even more prevalent in the measurement of quality. Centers are consistently wrapped up in the overall "average" scoring of their agents and fail to get to the interaction detail, which is where they can make the biggest difference. Large-scale improvement is made in a call center by making changes and procedures that impact the most people. This is further improved by changing the largest number of people, one person at a time.

> Large-scale improvement is made in a call center by making changes and procedures that impact the most people.

Quality programs often fail to measure because they get wrapped up in the overall quality scoring. Then, they focus education only on those people who scored poorly overall. For example, in the following chart whom would you seek for further training?

	#1	#2	#3	#4	#5	#6	#7	#8	#9	#10	Total
Donald Duck	10.00	10.00	9.50	10.00	10.00	9.80	9.00	9.79	7.00	9.50	9.46
Mickey Mouse	9.50	10.00	9.50	9.50	9.50	9.50	9.50	9.50	7.00	9.00	9.25
Goofy	10.00	10.00	9.50	9.70	9.00	10.00	9.00	9.50	9.50	10.00	9.62
Pluto	9.00	10.00	9.00	10.00	9.00	9.00	9.00	9.00	9.00	9.00	9.20
Pinocchio	10.00	9.00	9.50	9.50	9.50	9.50	10.00	9.70	7.00	9.80	9.35
Captain Hook	5.00	4.00	8.00	9.50	9.00	10.00	9.00	6.00	7.00	9.00	7.65
Minnie Mouse	9.50	10.00	9.50	4.00	9.50	9.50	10.00	10.00	10.00	10.00	9.20
Total	9.00	9.00	9.21	8.89	9.36	9.61	9.36	9.07	8.07	9.47	

At first glance, it is obvious that Captain Hook is the poorest performer. He has the lowest overall total score and is the person that needs focus. Most call centers have the horizontal scoring (left to right totals) well thought out and under control, whether they are automated or not. They all do some form of scoring, and most centers can give you an overall ranking of their people. They have found some ways to measure quality and measure the overall score.

World-class call centers that are focused on quality look vertically as well as horizontally. They value the overall scores but they dig deeper as well. They would see two more issues. First, they seek out Minnie Mouse and find what her issue is with Question #4. You would miss her poor performance on Question #4 if you did not focus on the individual questions. World-class call centers focus on the details. Her improvement in this area will improve her overall score and the score of the team.

The second area that world-class call centers would focus on is Question #9. This question has overall poor performance. With improvement, this area could positively affect the entire organization. Once again, a focus on the individual questions makes for improvement in the call center.

World-class call centers have an additional challenge if they are part of enterprise organizations, or companies with multiple call centers. In order to be successful they need to meet the same standards all around the world. This adds additional challenges in reporting. This same type of reporting at one center must be able to add up at the enterprise level. This ability to take the data to the enterprise level will produce substantial improvement.

An enterprise example would be as follows:

ABC Corporation

Location	Quality Score	Productivity Score	Adherence
Ledyard, CT	9.1	94%	93%
Kingston, RI	8.4	89%	94%
Dallas, TX	7.6	81%	94%
La Jolla, CA	9.5	93%	92%
Orlando, FL	9.3	90%	96%
Boulder, CO	9.2	93%	95%
Total	8.85	90%	94%

Now you have the information that is important to you available in one report. Many years ago, I worked with Mike Maloney, who created a call center report that he called an EYEWATKOASR report. It was: "Everything You Ever Wanted to Know on a Single Report report!"

In the best of worlds you could go from this report and begin to peel away the information to look at the center, teams, and ultimately, individuals to see where your successes or failures were. Also of note is the fact that many centers will make their productivity score some combination of factors within their measurements.

Reports With Layers

One of the other failures of vendors and information systems departments today is that their reporting programs fail to tell stories. Effective reporting tells a story of what happened. With the advent of crystal reports and open databases, the best feature of reporting is that you can "create your own reports." The "good ole days" of a detailed reporting package that told a story have, for the most part, been forgotten. A great reporting package tells a story by peeling away the layers of the problem until you get to the root of it. Great reporting should read like an organization chart.

> A great reporting package tells a story by peeling away the layers of the problem until you get to the root of it.

Organization Chart Reporting

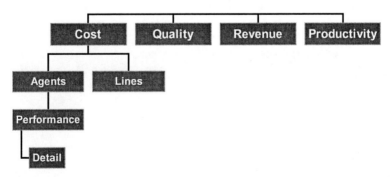

It starts with cost, quality, productivity, and revenue. These would be the top levels of an organization! Did the area measured have a positive or negative impact on one of these areas?

Next, it goes into more detail based on the level of the report. It peels away layers until you get to the individual agent and to the root of the problem. We are constantly focused at the system/enterprise/group level and with the individual.

Quality reporting without a reference or comparison to productivity data leaves us feeling like something is missing. The combination of both pieces of data can be a major benefit to your organization. Do you have a set of reports that matches up quality and productivity?

Quality reporting has the capability to tell an executive virtually everything that he or she needs to know about an organization. It has the potential to factor in all areas of the call center. Take a look at the critical questions that you have in your call center. I guarantee you that quality measurement can give you more information to help you solve your problems. Try it!

> Quality reporting has the capability to tell an executive virtually everything that he or she needs to know about an organization.

When we were all very young, we used to get report cards that had a lot more detail. Not only did we get a score, but we also received behavior scores, and the teacher always wrote a note at the end of each grading period. The note was always read by my parents to me. It added a personal, real-live witness account of my performance. Over time it added to the numbers by telling more of the story. As we grew older, those went away in junior high, high school, and college. We received our grades or numbers, and that was the end of the story. Do you think your business or team would run better if the reports that you circulated were more valuable? We have eyewitness live accounts of what happens each day, week, and month. Why don't we use them? Why not make your reports come alive? Make them tell the story and help you to make better decisions.

WRAP-UP

- Reports can be a useful measurement tool that helps you identify the strengths and weaknesses of your department.

- Interactive details can provide insights into many areas of a call center. Used along with averages, they give a clear picture of what is happening around you.

- The best reports include layers of information that allow you to identify the exact cause of a problem.

CHAPTER 22: THE ISSUE OF PRIVACY

Government Involvement

The practice of electronically monitoring calls, so essential to our industry, brings up an issue that we must all be aware of today. That is, the government regulation of electronic monitoring and privacy in the workplace. It's an issue that affects us all and will continue to do so.

> You only need to have one person in a sales or service center whose voice or data you want to monitor for privacy to be significant to you.

In 1993, I had the privilege of working with government officials and industry leaders on this critical issue. The government had created the Senate Subcommittee for Electronic Monitoring and Privacy in the Workforce, headed by former Senator Paul Simon (D-IL). It was one of the earliest attempts by the government to be active in call centers.

First I testified for the Senate Subcommittee on the bill and then I worked closely with all parties to come up with a legislation that would work for the industry. The statement I made to the subcommittee is included in the Appendix at the end of the book.

It was a fascinating experience, and very telling when it comes to the issues of privacy. What was unfortunate was the fact that the government decided to merge a couple of issues regarding privacy: call center monitoring and video cameras in nurses' bathrooms.

To be connected with video cameras in nurses' bathrooms seemed pretty ridiculous, yet the issues of privacy run deep in many industries. For our business, it affects the company, supervisors, customers, and naturally, the telephone agents. It is rare now to hear a voice announcement in a call center that doesn't start with the statement, "Your call may be monitored or recorded for quality purposes."

147

Amazingly, nine years later, we are still dealing with the same issues. Now, the privacy matter has extended beyond telephone calls to include e-mails and Web chat. However, the principles that we put forward in 1993 still hold true.

Existing Guidelines

Single and Dual Consent States

First, remember any call center that voice records or monitors is located in a single or dual consent state. In a single consent state, only one side of the conversation needs to know they are being recorded. For example, if you call me in Texas and I know that I am recording you or that my company is recording our call, it is single consent.

In a dual consent state, both parties must be aware of the recording. That is why you hear the disclaimer at the beginning of calls to toll-free numbers that often says, "Your call may be monitored for quality purposes."

Some states, like Georgia, have additional requirements such as putting a symbol in the phone book and registration to identify monitoring.

> In a single consent state, only one side of the conversation needs to know they are being recorded. In a dual consent state, both parties must be aware of the recording.

The Nixon administration got in trouble because it was recording two people, and neither one of them knew about it. Linda Tripp recently got in trouble in the state of Maryland with Monica Lewinsky over dual consent issues. (That is twice in one book with a Monica Lewinsky reference!)

Checks and Balances

Make sure that you monitor the monitors. This is a very important practice that all companies should enforce for their own protection. Monitoring the monitor can easily reduce the potential for conflict, discrimination, and error. Your company should review the scoring, use of the information, scheduling, and selection criteria of the people doing the monitoring. Make sure you have a plan and set of rules in place to review your monitors. Power and information can have a strange effect on some people. Make sure you have the correct checks and balances in place for your monitors.

Personal Calls

Monitoring may be used only for business purposes. Don't monitor personal calls! Don't let your supervisors or monitors record, save, or talk about personal calls. They will hear them. It's inevitable. Make sure you have strict rules to stop the recording when a personal call has been monitored and immediately erase the call. I know many of you are thinking, "What if we tell them no personal calls and we hear one?" Work with your HR department to find out how to handle it. In any case, if a supervisor hears a personal call that has been recorded, make sure the supervisor is trained to stop listening and either hold for HR or eliminate the call. The damage and risk to your business as well as your relationship with your employees far exceed any information you might use to catch one individual.

> Don't monitor personal calls! Don't let your supervisors or monitors record, save, or talk about personal calls.

Fairness

All similarly situated employees must be monitored consistently. In other words, you cannot monitor one group only in the morning when they are well rested and monitor another group only late in the day. This is very important from a fairness standpoint.

Make sure you take a random sampling of all calls that will give you the best perspective on the employees' performance. It also will eliminate any discriminatory risks that may occur if you are operating inconsistently from one group to the other.

Disclosure

Disclosure must be made to employees regarding the substance of the monitoring. In other words, you must tell them what quantitative and qualitative factors are being evaluated and how those factors are interrelated. It is important that you tell your people *exactly* why you are monitoring them and how you are going to evaluate the information. This is especially true if you are using the information for any sort of compensation.

149

> It is important that you tell your people exactly why
> you are monitoring them and how you are going to
> evaluate the information.

Monitoring must be disclosed, but restraints, especially any time restraints, must have enough flexibility to avoid destroying the accuracy and reliability of the information collected. You can use signs, offer letters, reminders, updates, charts, written plans, etc. to tell your agents what type of monitoring you are doing. It is smart legally, relationally, and financially for you to do this. Don't make it a secret.

Storage

Data and information in whatever form (visual, audio, etc.) must be recorded, stored, and made available for the protection of the employee and the employer for a reasonable period of time. A reasonable period of time should be 30 to 180 days. Technology has changed the need to save unheard calls used solely for monitoring.

If you don't have the time to listen and score the call, then why not erase it and get a new one? If you are going to keep the calls, you should save them for a publicized period of time and be consistent. Don't keep the same type of calls (for training purposes, disciplinary purposes, etc.) for different periods of times. Use one standard to determine how long all calls will be kept.

New Areas of Monitoring

This cannot be said strongly enough: Expect that the same types of experiences we have had with voice will also occur with all the other types of media in a customer service and sales center. Privacy and electronic monitoring are issues your company will have to deal with over the next 50 years and more. It will become an increasingly larger issue because it is rapidly moving out of only a few areas, such as the call centers, and into the enterprises themselves. If the federal government won't make changes, then the states will. Expect ongoing legislation, new reform, and a constant battle over what constitutes someone's privacy.

> Expect that the same types of experiences that we have
> had with voice will also occur with all the other types
> of media in a customer service and sales center.

150

The benefits of monitoring technology in the enterprise will be substantial as companies look for new ways to increase productivity. At the same time, as monitoring technology reaches throughout the enterprise, you can expect increases in litigation and abuse.

WRAP-UP

- The issue of privacy has created several important guidelines for monitoring calls electronically.

- It is important to adhere to the existing guidelines so that your company, your agents, and your customers are protected.

- Advances in technology and new types of transactions will ensure that privacy remains an important issue in our industry.

Chapter 23: The Perfect Call Center

A Collection of Greatness

You see it in sports all of the time. The experts try to figure out what the perfect athlete would be like. The arm of Joe Namath, the scrambling ability of Roger Staubach, the grace under pressure of Joe Montana, the accuracy of Troy Aikman. If we could just bring all these unique attributes together, we could create the perfect quarterback.

Over the last twenty years, I have had seen many call centers. Every one of them is unique in its own way. From large to small, many have exciting technologies and opportunities. I have decided to combine the outstanding qualities I have seen to create the perfect call center. Each of the qualities listed below was chosen for a specific reason. I am sure that I missed some great call centers, but the ones listed below can certainly hold their own against any in the world.

Attributes of the Perfect Call Center

The perfect call center would have:

The Quality Compensation Plans of Blue Cross / Blue Shield of Alabama

I mentioned the creativity of the group at Blue Cross/ Blue Shield of Alabama in a previous chapter. They have found a successful way of combining quality performance with compensation and have achieved results. This is a very well-run customer service organization. Like all of these companies, they are worth visiting.

The Vision of Ford Motor Company Business Assistance Center

These folks get it. They run a world-class call center in their Detroit facility. Ford is consistently a leader in all areas of its business. They have stayed on the leading edge in innovation and in employer-employee relationships. The Ford Assistance Center is stellar-looking as well.

The Creativity of IBM Corporation

I have told you about IBM's creativity in earlier chapters. It doesn't stop with bingo and valet car parking. They compile new ways to motivate, reward, and train their people. It is not beyond them to have cruises and vacations combined with quarterly award and recognition programs. There is always something new at IBM. On a side note, their Dallas facility is one of the nicest call centers I have ever been in.

The Interaction Detail Reporting of General Electric

You wouldn't think that the sophisticated policies for quality of Jack Welch would work in the triage necessity of the MASH units we refer to as call centers. But you would be wrong. GE sets the standard for quality in all areas of their business. When it happens, they measure it, make changes, and improve it. Their ability to run enterprise call centers working together is unparalleled in the industry.

The On Purpose Focus of eTelecare

To be world class requires focus and being on purpose about your strategy. This company manages quality through a proprietary performance management system, which affords supervisors the opportunity to spend 70 percent of their time coaching customer service associates. Another differentiator at eTelecare is the fact the company hires only graduates from top universities in the Philippines and provides them with anywhere from six to 10 weeks of initial and client-specific training.

The Leading Edge Technology of Cigna Corporation

Being a world-class leader requires innovation, which sometimes means pushing the envelope. You wouldn't think that would be a healthcare company, but it is. Cigna makes bold decisions and extends their technology to better serve their customers and maintain a competitive advantage.

The Quality Evaluation Forms Process of American Express Europe

American Express Europe takes quality serious. They continue to make innovative changes to the type of quality measurement they do. They stretch technology through database management and reporting to find answers and advantages in the servicing of their customers.

The Training Programs of Telvista

Telvista's focus on training and career development has produced team members with unparalleled customer-service skills. Learning starts as soon as an agent walks in the front door and never stops. It's not surprising that this company, always on the leading edge of the contact center industry, would be an early adopter of e-learning software to close the loop on performance optimization.

The Management Leadership of AT&T Wireless

Managers are critical to success. There are none more talented and prepared than the folks at AT&T Wireless. I have met them around the country, and they are always professional and prepared. I wouldn't be surprised if many of them end up being the next leaders of call centers around the country.

The Desktop Toys (Employee Motivation) of Nintendo

It sounds strange, but every representative at Nintendo gets a set of all the toys and games at their workstations. Most call centers try like crazy to keep any and all distractions away from the agents. At Nintendo, their games are their products, and up-to-date and empowered agents means great service to their customers.

The Exchange of Information at the Orange County Register (OCR)

Call centers that get everyone involved with the enterprise make an impact on the success of the company. Enterprise collaboration is an important part of OCR's CRM initiative and reinforces the Pulitzer Prize-winning paper's core value of integrity. If customers share their feelings on certain promotions or comment on particular ads, that information is sent to marketing. The paper has even instituted programs requiring every director—including the CEO—to review customer contacts on a regular basis to give them a better understanding of their subscriber base.

The Real-Time Reporting of Dell Corporation

Vendors spend a lot of time trying to make technology do more than a customer could ever want it to do. Dell Computers is one of the few places that can never get enough out of their vendor software. They are always improving and innovating. Vendors regularly show up to find their products and software providing value and benefits to Dell that they hadn't even thought of yet. Dell stretches the vendors to get real-time advantage for their customers. It makes them world-class.

The Hiring Strategy of ADP Corporation

ADP Corporation was one of the very first companies to recognize how important the hiring part of the marketplace really is. It has one of the most sophisticated and successful enterprise hiring strategies in the world. They are on purpose with technology, process, and decision-making for hiring talented people for their call centers. If you want to learn how to hire people, ADP is the place to go.

The Vendor Relationship Strategy of The Boeing Corporation

There is not a Web site in any strong company in the world that doesn't have a partner's section. Without partnerships, you can't survive in business today. Boeing recognizes the importance of vendor relationships. They have done an excellent job of helping the vendors understand their goals and direction. This gives them willing accomplices in achieving their goals. Vendors must be partners if companies are to be successful today. Any other position that you put them in is a disadvantage to you in the marketplace.

The Planning of Convergys Corporation

Everyone knows their responsibility at this company. The agents know their roles and how they are reviewed and compensated. The managers know exactly what their responsibility is and how they are compensated. When everyone knows their role and what is expected of them, you get excellence.

The People Scheduling at Georgia Power

Georgia Power has two centers, with 300 plus people in different locations, and the customers get served with world-class support. Earlier in the book we talked about scheduling and its importance in the hierarchy of a call center's needs. The reason Georgia Power excels at customer satisfaction is because it has this part down.

The real-time training at Kaiser Permanente

Large, sophisticated companies have large and sophisticated challenges when it comes to training and keeping customer service representatives up to date on the myriad of changes that need to be made. Kaiser does this very well in large quantity right at the rep's desktop.

The Recognition of Opportunity at Tucson Electric

Tucson Electric Power Company (TEP) isn't just reading its customers' meters. The utility is measuring itself when it comes to the delivery of quality customer service, because not only does the company want to generate power, it wants to generate a favorable impression. The company handles 3,000 customer calls per day, and as management has wisely surmised, that's 3,000 opportunities per day to create or reinforce a favorable opinion of TEP. Considering the company is likely to face competition as a result of deregulation, quality has become a key component in TEP's strategy to build a better brand and enhance its image with customers.

The Telephone Skills of Budget Rent-a-Car

Check out their customer sales skills. The reps on the phones get it. They are professional, well-trained and enthusiastic. This is very hard to do well in one place, never mind in centers around the country. Your most valuable asset is your people. World-class centers have world-class people on the phones.

Creating Your Own Perfect Call Center

After reading this list, you probably have a pretty good idea of what it takes to be a world-class call center. How far away are you? Use the resources available to you to measure your center. Then, identify the areas that need improvement and get busy. Remember that it is always the "jets" at the company who have the vision and audacity to make a difference in their jobs. You are merely one or two actions away from making a difference in your company and soaring to success.

WRAP-UP

- The perfect call center has many attributes. How many of them does your center already possess?

- Any one area of greatness can make your call center world class. More than one can make it absolutely phenomenal.

157

Section Five

Technology to Increase Productivity

CHAPTER 24: DEPOSITS AND WITHDRAWALS

Viewing Transactions as Collisions

Call center, contact center, CRM center, customer center, phone area, Web-contact, E-connection… there will be more names! Whenever we have one of "these" centers, we have thousands of interactions, each with three distinct parts. You have a customer/prospect, a company (agent/Web chatter/service/sales agent), and the activity itself, which ultimately is a collision. The collision is inevitable, and I think that it is a very provocative way to look at the interaction.

A collision is defined as:

1. The act or process of colliding; a crash or conflict.

2. *Physics.* A brief dynamic event consisting of the close approach of two or more particles, such as atoms, resulting in an abrupt change of momentum or exchange of energy.

When you have a collision between people, one of the parties can be hurt. The pain or risk of something going wrong is tied to how well both sides are prepared for the collision. Because we have so many customers from so many different walks of life, we (the call centers) really have to do the preparation for both sides. It is our responsibility. Think of it like a car colliding with a bicycle. We are the car. When we have the collision with the bicycle, we need to make sure that no damage occurs.

In our types of collisions, however, we need to worry about more than just damage. We need to make sure that the customer actually enjoys the collision. But we shouldn't stop there. We need to go even further and attempt to exceed the customers' expectations while we solve their problems.

> In our types of collisions, however, we need to worry about more than just damage. We need to make sure that the customer actually enjoyed the collision.

161

A Case Study in Meeting Expectations

I recently purchased a Dell laptop computer via the phone. I had gone online to find a laptop and wanted to wait for the best deal. This went on for weeks. I finally decided that I needed the laptop quickly. I was going out of town and wanted to have it before the weekend. The Web couldn't help me with my extra requirement to have it by the weekend, so I needed to find a person who could help me. Online ordering could speed shipment (ground, air, overnight) but couldn't guarantee or tell me when it would be ready to ship. So I went to the trusted telephone.

After going through four levels of VRU, my call was answered by someone named Shannon who asked: "What can I help you build?" I gave her all the information and told her my key issue was delivery by Friday. She assured me that she could work it out for me so my laptop came when I wanted it. She told me that this was something the company couldn't do through its Web site. She also put me on hold and confirmed with her supervisor that laptops shipped immediately, so I would get it in time. Let me be clear that she never guaranteed it would come, only that she had checked with her supervisor. The supervisor confirmed that it was an item that was usually shipped the day following the order, and they both agreed I would get it in time.

Her recommended configuration was almost $150 dollars better than the Web site recommendation. I asked her about the difference, and she said that sometimes there is a difference. We went over the details twice.

Fast forward with me to a week and a half later. The computer didn't come early, and I had to add an additional piece of software for $107. The computer is great and I really love it, but I feel Dell let me down three times—missing the delivery date, the inaccuracy of the order, and the follow-up service.

I had spent months on the Web looking for the best deal. Most laptops are very comparable in price. I specifically purchased the Dell product because of the company's excellent reputation for service. I had a predisposition that Dell had great customer service. My expectations were that Dell would be amazing as a vendor.

What is interesting is that my call was anonymous when we started. I didn't expect to deal with the same person after that initial call. However, after ordering, Shannon became my direct sales representative. I purchased the product on a Wednesday night. I was told it would arrive on Friday. When it didn't arrive on Friday, I called Shannon back. Dell is incredibly thorough about sending a list of what was on the order and all of sales representative's information in case you need to get in touch with him or her again if I needed to. Shannon, my sales representative, didn't work on Friday or Saturday and would return Monday. Her voicemail directed me to a VRU, which told me where my laptop was. It was in production. I called back in and talked to a different sales representative, who was unable to access my account or provide any additional information. He tried for a while and then transferred me to customer service. The queue time in customer service was 11 minutes. I left messages for Shannon most of the weekend, but didn't hear from her.

A few points here:

- I didn't ask for a personal salesperson. They gave me one anyway. Sometimes this is great, your own personalized service. In this instance, it was a detriment due to my time constraints and the fact that the agent that the system randomly connected me to wasn't working when I needed her.

- I didn't ask to have my service handled by a VRU. I received personal service for the sale. When I needed support, it was either a VRU or a queue time that I was unwilling to wait for. I could have also received service from the person that I originally talked to, but she was unavailable. Perhaps better answers were on the other end of the 11-minute wait time, but that was too long for me to wait, and I had already missed my weekend deadline.

- The Web service was no different from the call center service in price or delivery, despite what the agent told me.

My first impression of Dell was that it was not an "amazing" service organization. I started with an expectation that my service experience would be awesome. My initial personal dealings with Dell on this issue were not very positive at all. I kept the laptop. What is unusual is that somewhere down in my deep "consumer subconscious" the following thoughts ran through my mind:

- The people who told me they have had great service were really bright people and wouldn't steer me wrong.

- I wanted a Dell PC. I liked the way it looked. The price wasn't less, but it wasn't more either. I could have cancelled my PC over the weekend. I didn't.

- I had this strange impression that if I went somewhere else the service would be worse.

- Dell is considered one of the best customer service organizations in the world.

Is the answer "You can't please all the people all of the time?" I don't think so. I was pre-disposed to having an excellent experience and I didn't. Right now I have an awesome PC that is really great but it was not what I expected.

Keeping Score of Deposits and Withdrawals

In any relationship, personal or business, there are deposits and withdrawals. When we have positive experiences, we make deposits. Negative experiences are withdrawals. It is imperative that we keep our deposits consistently coming in to make up for the inevitable withdrawals that will occur. Dell had "deposits" with me, and I had no experience with the company. The deposits Dell had made with other people made a difference with me. These deposits made enough of a difference that it kept me with the product when we had a tough time.

> In any relationship, personal or business, there are deposits and withdrawals. It is imperative that we keep our deposits consistently coming in to make up for the inevitable withdrawals that will occur.

Let's break down my experience and see how it compares with your company and call center experience.

Step	Deposit/Withdrawal
Previous reputation	Deposit
Web site	Deposit
Web site (Quick Ship failure)	Withdrawal
Web site Point/Click failure	Withdrawal
Customer telephone option	Deposit
VRU Prompts (4)	Withdrawal

164

Step	**Deposit/Withdrawal**
Individual salesperson	Deposit
Positive answer to shipment	Deposit
Better price than on web	Deposit
Follow-up e-mail with contacts	Deposit
Error in order	Withdrawal
Salesperson unavailable	Withdrawal
Customer service wait time	Withdrawal
No return call from salesperson	Withdrawal
Delayed delivery date	Withdrawal
How I felt when I got product	Deposit
Performance of product	Deposit
Feeling of Value for the Product	Deposit

Yes, Dell won. I still have the product but have not called back for additional service. I haven't had to call.

When we buy something we have a tendency to do a "Benjamin Franklin," in which we measure the pluses and the minuses, then make our decisions. I would rather use and evaluate products, and for that matter, sell in an environment that uses a "baseball game." I like the fact that there are nine innings or factors. This works with the Harvard University concept of seven plus or minus two items.

Second, I like that fact that you can score more than one run in an inning. This makes it possible to buy the product or systems that don't have the most features or least price but instead have the items that are most important to you. We discussed this earlier when we focused on providing services to your customers that they value. The Dell reputation and the quality of the product scored more runs than some of the failures.

I love my Dell laptop. It has worked perfectly so far, and I am really pleased with it.

Every interaction that you do as a company does matter. What you do with each customer throughout the relationship will matter and will matter for a very long time. Looking at an interaction from a deposits and withdrawals viewpoint will help you see the areas where you can make a difference and those that you will just have to struggle through. Keep in mind that even a perfect transaction in a call center will have both deposits and withdrawals. An example of a certain deposit will be a great price. An example of a certain withdrawal would be a long VRU menu!

> Looking at an interaction from a deposits and withdrawals viewpoint will help you see the areas where you can make a difference and those that you will just have to struggle through.

Our call centers and our businesses naturally make deposits and withdrawals with customers. How is your call center doing? Are you flush with deposits or on the verge of bankruptcy?

Sometimes it can be difficult to determine what our deposits and withdrawals are. In fact, our perceptions of them can be quite different than our customer's. How can you find out how the customer views his or her collision with you? Technology—the third basic element of a call center—can help. In the next chapter, we will discuss a useful tool that can tell you if you have more deposits or withdrawals.

WRAP-UP

- Transactions in a call center are like collisions. The more we understand this, the better prepared we will be.

- All interactions are made up of positive experiences (deposits) and negative experiences (withdrawals). Make sure you make more deposits than withdrawals.

- Customers arrive with expectations both positive and negative. That is the reason you work so hard to build a great reputation. Like Dell it starts you off with deposits!

The Importance of Customer Feedback

Have you noticed that the number of award shows in the entertainment industry seems to be growing? Every year there are more than the year before. Out of all of these shows, the ones that I think are most telling are the people's choice awards. After all, they are the ones that get right down to the bottom line—what do the people think? Isn't that what really matters?

If there were a people's choice award for call centers, how would you fare? Would your customers cast a vote for you, or are you making too many withdrawals and not enough deposits to win their votes? Perhaps you should ask them and see.

Many call centers today measure their performance based mostly on internal information. This means that they combine productivity information with internal quality programs to gauge agents' performance. The failure of this process is not in the effort.

> Much time is spent to gather, quantify, and collate the information. The part that is missing is the customer input.

As an industry, we generally want and try to discover our customers' feelings and opinions. We just go about it in the wrong way. Most companies fail to consider the customer input on an individual basis. Instead, they search and invest in an "overall" customer feeling. To achieve success, quality programs must include the customers' perception of the agent in the same quantity as the internal evaluations. Anything less will provide skewed results.

Survey Shortcomings

While crisscrossing the country, you will inevitably find hundreds, if not thousands, of different surveys being conducted by companies. You find them in hotel rooms, airplanes, anywhere on the Web, cable installations, and fast food restaurants. Call centers are no different.

We have a myriad of ways to survey our clients, including telephone surveys, Web surveys, mail-in surveys, e-mail surveys, and in-call and after-call surveys. The combined brainpower of the corporate call center world focused on "asking the right question, over the right sampling, and in the right time frame" could probably get us to the moon and back by next Thursday.

These survey results have a tremendous potential to solve all sorts of problems and help companies make key decisions. I have nothing against surveying. Surveying is a smart business idea with tremendous potential, yet its full potential in the call center is coming up short.

> One of the key ingredients to a successful call center is being missed all around the world. That key ingredient is the customer feedback to the individual agent.

Call centers have mastered getting some sort of response back to their companies. They have, in many instances, gotten feedback for the individual centers and, in some rare instances, to the agents themselves. The challenge is that the feedback to individual agents is not an ongoing part of the performance improvement of the call center.

In today's call centers, monitoring programs are set up to measure somewhere between 5 and 12 calls per agent per month. In those centers that utilize Web chat or e-mail, there may be some review of these interactions as well. These reviews, combined with some sort of productivity data, are used to measure and improve the performance of the individual.

At most call centers, this data is also used to help determine incentive compensation. This data can include many different evaluations. It may include reviews from the supervisor, a quality manager, trainer, another representative, and sometimes an outside consulting firm. Still, there is one critical component missing—the customer. What did the customer think of that call and that agent? This information combined with all of the other internal information can make a huge difference.

Immediate Response Surveys

A healthcare industry study examined the perception of customers and companies focused on the soft skills of the call. These skills include professionalism, courtesy, confidence, and enthusiasm. What the study found was that the company and the customer had two very different views of the agents' soft skills. However, the customers and the companies usually agreed on other factors, such as accuracy, information given, and results.

We must involve the customer in both parts of the equation. It is not enough to simply survey after the fact for an overview of the call. We must get customers' specific feedback to the agent quickly after the call.

The solution lies in a different kind of performance measurement. The equation must include a sampling of calls that are monitored by the company and a sampling of calls that are monitored by the customer for the individual agent. These two combined will give us the results we need.

This type of measurement can be accomplished using a number of different technologies. Most performance monitoring systems provide a vehicle to record the call or interaction for review. Even live monitoring (I'm not sure why any large organization would still do this as the cornerstone to evaluating agents) provides us an opportunity to capture the interaction.

The next step requires an immediate feedback mechanism for the customer. An after-call survey is the most efficient. In this type of measurement, the customer is asked prior to the call to wait until the call has concluded for a short survey. Statistics show that approximately 20 to 30 percent of the people offered the opportunity would stay on the line for the survey.

> With computer telephony integration as the cornerstone, we can record the call and then record the customer's perception right at the time of the interaction.

It is important that your systems are designed to conduct these recordings by individual agent. This will enable you to get the feedback to the agent.

One tremendous benefit of this is that you have the information at your immediate disposal. You know instantly if you have made more deposits or withdrawals and can take immediate action. If there is an outstanding problem, this method allows you to transfer the call back to the agent or a supervisor to resolve the matter immediately. It would not take very many "saved" customers to reap the rewards of your investment.

Additionally, your company could page supervisors, salespeople, or send instant e-mails with the results. Can you imagine having a senior executive call a customer back within 10 minutes of a poor survey? Now we are talking Customer Relationship Management!

This same result could be achieved through instant e-mail or an outbound call. It is critical that you capture the customer's input as soon as possible after the call. The fast response gains you the most insight and the truest picture of what actually occurred.

It seems so simple yet is missed most often. We provide service for our customers' satisfaction. We do this with a group of people that we measure and review, sometimes better than any other area of our organization.

Our customers want better service. We have a desire to give that to them. We must make the connection between the two groups—the agents and the customers–at the point of contact if we want to succeed. To collect this information without taking full advantage of the benefits is an incredible waste of money and customer goodwill.

WRAP-UP

- Customer feedback is essential to any performance measurement program. It can be obtained through a variety of surveying methods.

- Immediate response surveys allow companies to address problems quickly and provide specific feedback to individual agents.

- If there is an outstanding problem, this method allows you to transfer the call back to the agent to resolve the matter immediately.

CHAPTER 26: EXPECTATIONS

First Impressions

Recently I stayed at the Four Seasons Hotel in Washington, D.C. From the moment that I arrived, it was obvious that I was dealing with a company that understood customer service. The bellman almost fell over trying to help me in the building (not a pest, but genuinely happy to see me!). Once I was inside, the three desk clerks said they would help me as soon as they were finished with the customers they were servicing.

Great customer service doesn't necessarily mean that you never wait. Having to wait is inevitable at most great hotels, restaurants, and theme parks. The key is how aware the employees are at these waiting moments and what proactive actions they take.

I want to contrast my experience at the Washington, D.C. Four Seasons with a recent trip to the Doral in Miami, Florida. This is a very high-class and successful hotel as well. When I walked in, three people were standing behind the counter working on their computers with their heads down. No one was in line. If you have ever waited in line at an airport, you know that you never commit to one of the people unless you make eye contact with him or her. If you don't make eye contact, the agent could spend more time finishing up his or her last task, and the person behind you could get the "true" next available person.

After about a minute or so, I walked right up and stood in front of two of them. They still didn't look up for more than another minute. I was standing less than three feet from them! I moved back in line and stood there for another three minutes. It had become a test of wills and I was losing! Finally, one of the people looked up, smiled, and said, "May I help you?"

Should I have said something immediately? Should I have said something after I walked up and stood in front of them or when I moved back in line? It is not my nature to scream or make a scene. How long is the appropriate time to wait and then request help? Does my level of patience make a difference to the hotel?

I was offended, disappointed, and felt like I wasn't important. I didn't tell anyone there. It was late at night, and I just wanted my room. I did tell the ten or so people I was with that weekend. This one experience affected the remainder of my stay at this otherwise great resort.

The first of several lessons that can be learned here is to get off to a great start with your customers. First impressions really do make a difference. They can shape your customers' perceptions for years to come.

> First impressions really do make a difference. They can shape your customers' perceptions for years to come.

This is especially true in your call center.

First impressions are based on customers' expectations. By meeting those expectations, you can make a great impression. However, customer service is complicated because every one of your customers has a different expectation about the type of support he or she should receive. This expectation can be a killer when you are trying to provide quality service.

New Technologies, New Expectations

To top it off, expectations are always changing. Meeting these expectations has never been more challenging than it is today as the number of options available to customers continues to grow. Yesterday, there were storefronts, call centers, and voice response. Today, we have added e-mail and Web chat. This means two new areas of expectations and challenges to meet.

> Expectations are always changing. Meeting these expectations has never been more challenging than it is today as the number of options available to customers continues to grow.

With variety comes complication and the risk of not making a good first impression. Web chat is an excellent example of not getting off on the right foot. I have already seen too many instances where the wait times and product quality is unacceptable. Let me give you an example.

I had a Palm V and I needed support. After fooling around with Palm's Web site, I chose the Web chat option Palm offered. For the past year, Web chat has been consistently growing as a support option for customers. Web chat is still a new communication procedure for companies. It has the same number of challenges as voice communication, only the challenges are different. (Note: One cool thing is that unlike a phone call, the Web chat conversation was there for me to copy to my hard drive!)

The wait time for the Web chat site was 45 minutes. Earlier I complained about a 13-minute wait from Dell. If you provided a 45-minute service response for a voice call, you would be considered a company that provided very poor customer service.

The following is a copy of my Web chat with a Palm customer service representative. Note the areas that I have bolded.

Rich:	Thank you for contacting Palm Incorporated. If you would like Palm to have a record of this, I will need your name, home telephone number, serial number, and type of Palm. A record of this chat will be logged under your telephone number.
Rich:	My name is Rich, how can I assist you today?
Michael:	This was way too long to wait!
Rich:	I am sorry. We have been terribly busy.
Michael:	My problem is that my wife and I both have a Palm pilot. She has one of the little ones and I have a Palm V.
Rich:	How can I help you?
Michael:	She uses Microsoft Outlook and I use the Palm software that comes with the system. Right now we have to use two computers because they won't reside on the same systems. Is there a device that I can hook to my pc that will allow us to both sync from the same port? Is there a way to synch to one program for one and one to the other?
Rich:	Yes, you are using Windows?

Michael:	is it possible for us to have two Outlook programs and have us both sync separately? Yes, I have Windows 98 on one machine and ME on the other.
Rich:	If you set up different profiles in Windows, you can sync to different applications.
Michael:	Is there a connector that plugs into the back of the machine that has two interfaces to the two different Palms? It would be a hassle to have to constantly swap cables.
Rich:	I have seen them but we do not make any.
Michael:	Can you send me directions on how to do this? Where could I get the cable?
Rich:	**I can't. I can only specify things about hardware made by Palm. Palm does not like me telling you about other company's products.**
Michael:	Can you send me directions on how to use my Palm with your software and my wife's smaller Palm with Outlook on the same machine?
Rich:	**I can't send you anything. I don't have e-mail capabilities.**
Michael:	Are you able to do more than one chat at a time?
Rich:	Yes, I am required to.
Michael:	How many are you doing at once?
Rich:	**Four right now**.
Michael:	Wow! Where do I get the instructions from?
Rich:	I don't know of a place offhand that illustrates multiple user profiles in Windows.
Michael:	Soooooo???? Anyone there?
Rich:	Yes, I am here.
Michael:	Should I cancel out because you can't help me? Where should I go to get the information? Is there somewhere else I can ask?

Rich: I am trying to help you; I am searching to find information you can reference about Windows.

Palm does not have any information about how to use Windows.

Michael: Thanks I appreciate your help

Rich: This may take a little time to find.

Michael: Should I wait?

Rich: If you want.

Michael: Do I have an option?

Rich: Yes.

Michael: Okay, I'm listening.

Rich: I have looked through microsoft.com and have not found a real clear picture but I will explain it to you. Since this chat has taken more than 20 minutes Palm would like a record of it. Can I have the information listed at the beginning of the chat?

Michael: What information is that?

Rich: Thank you for contacting Palm Incorporated. If you would like Palm to have a record of this, I will need your name, home telephone number, serial number, and type of Palm. A record of this chat will be logged under your telephone number.

Michael   (I gave him my information.)

Rich: What multiple users in Windows does is create separate preferences but the same base programs. This allows you to have separate programs for each user. To set multiple users up you need to go into the control panel and open Users. Just follow the prompts. To access this user click on start and go to log off. Change the name listed and hit enter. Now you are in the other profile. This allows you to switch the program you are syncing to. To get back to the original file just log off and change the name back.

> In the new profile you will need to install Pocket Mirror to allow the hot sync between the Palm and Outlook.

Michael: The new profile will actually be the Palm v and your software.

Rich: Okay. Then install and choose return to the Palm desktop.

Michael: Thanks, I will give it a try.

Rich: You are welcome.

Michael: Bye

Rich: Good bye. Thank you for contacting Palm Incorporated.

> Contact was closed by Rich.

This interaction took more than 20 minutes. If you look closely at what transpired, you will see that we really didn't get that much accomplished. There is much to learn about this type of communication method.

Here are some thoughts:

- The very first comment that was sent was a pre-arranged opening comment by the Palm representative. It was not friendly enough, and he started with another salutation right after the impersonal one that he had pre-arranged.

- This transaction most likely took longer than a voice call, and the problem wasn't corrected.

- Notice all the typos and short cuts that both of us took with capitalization and spacing. Will this hold up years from now? It is the style of Web chat. Will companies continue to allow their agents to use incorrect capitalization and grammar?

- One of the reasons it took so long is that Rich had four conversations going at the same time. I didn't consider it to be quality service. My wait was 45 minutes right out of the gate, and it was way too long between responses from him.

- His single biggest failure was telling me that Palm doesn't want him to give out information that has nothing to do with him. This isn't his fault; it's the company's. This is compounded by the fact that he wasn't able to send e-mail, nor did he have access to any other support numbers.

- Corporate policy took over later in the call when after 20 minutes he had to get information from me. What a terrible time to be asking for data!

- You can see that because of the transaction delay (him talking to other chatters) I would ask more than one question between his responses, and he was least one question behind me most of the time. I waited a really long time for his responses. Most people don't know that he is chatting with other people. They just think he is slow.

- Did Palm ever catch this call, and did the company correct the problem? I doubt it. If they did, they never called me.

If this had been a voice call today in a world-class call center, it would have been graded as an "F." Policy would have changed, and people would be moving to correct this type of service. With Web chat and the newer offerings, there are still many bugs to be worked out and corrected.

I applaud Palm for adding additional ways for the customer to reach the company. Like most good ideas, they need to be followed by great processes.

WRAP-UP

- First impressions are lasting impressions. Make them good ones by constantly striving to meet your customers' expectations.

- New technologies have changed customers' expectations. Companies must implement processes that will meet these changing demands.

177

CHAPTER 27: A KILLER APPLICATION FOR THE WEB

A Look At Web Chat

Have you ever noticed how much easier it is to tear something down than to build it up? For example, finding the holes in Web chat is pretty easy. It is much more difficult to take a technology that has early challenges and find an application where it can really make a difference. Let's take serious look at Web chat and a new area where it can make a major difference in the success of your call center.

On paper, Web chat seems like a phenomenal opportunity to provide a new level of support and services to your clients. Call centers are under tremendous pressure to take advantage of the Web.

There isn't a seminar or trade show that doesn't list the potential of the Web and its impact on call centers. It sounds simple: customer service over the Web, real-time support without voice. As I have traveled around the country and spoken to Fortune 1000 companies, I have begun to realize the advantages and disadvantages of this technology.

Advantages

- If you are an e tailer or you sell services over the Web, Web chat is a mandatory service offering. Success has been limited, but when it occurs, it is great. In most instances, Web chat has not reduced telephone traffic.

- It is pretty cool, and it is the gateway to Voice Over Internet Protocol (VOIP) or an alternative to VOIP.

- The Web is the future, and companies inevitably need to "be in the game."

- Web chat will supplement the transactions that already exist. Although some have said that Web chat will replace VRUs, nothing could be further from the truth. Why would you move from automation back to people if the job is being done correctly?

Disadvantages

- If you aren't an e-tailer, Web chat could be a major hassle that most companies are trying to avoid or at least delay.

- Web chat costs much more than a phone call.

- It takes longer than most phone calls. Some say three times as long!

- It's cumbersome.

- Most companies have not deployed the technology that can make it better, such as e-mail connectivity, forms sharing, and Web collaboration.

- The biggest complaint is that it is another queue to worry about, another group to staff, train, and measure, as well as another area that has the potential to deliver poor service.

Work Support Management

I believe that there is tremendous opportunity to take advantage of Web chat and the power of this technology. One killer application that can help is Work Support Management (WSM). The location is right inside your call center.

Work Support Management is the delivery of technology and services internal to your CRM center to reduce cost and increase profitability. This is accomplished by taking advantage of the innate strengths of the Web and Web chat technology to reduce your costs and increase the performance of your call center.

> There is tremendous opportunity to take advantage of Web chat and the power of this technology. One killer application that can help is Work Support Management (WSM).

The benefits of WSM Web chat in your call center will be reduced talk time, reduction in transfers, increased up-selling, and a reduction in training costs.

One of the fastest growing technologies within a call center is instant messaging, such as AOL instant messaging. Many call centers that I have visited have instituted some sort of instant messaging for communications between the agents. The problem is that the intention of the messaging is to provide support, but what is occurring is a distraction to the agents. Additionally, there is no monitoring or control of the time and effort spent on instant messaging.

Web chat support is a superior support tool that is designed to reduce the reliance on Level Two personnel (the first level of support for the agents), improve training validation, and increase performance. This is accomplished by using the power of the Web to provide real-time support on the front lines of your call center.

> Web chat support is a superior support tool that is designed to reduce the reliance on Level Two personnel, improve training validation, and increase performance.

Requirements for Work Support Management

In order for Work Management Support to be really effective, it must be combined with other technologies. The following are the Web chat features that are optimal for Work Support Management to work properly.

Intelligent / Skills-Based Routing

This will enable the center to route calls to the WSM agent who can best provide support. These calls can be queued for the agent. It removes the randomness of instant messaging and queues the calls to the best available resource. (See the next chapter about skills-based routing.)

Full Duplex Messaging

This technology eliminates the need to press the Send button or wait for completion of the message. One can see the correspondence as it occurs. In an internal application, speed is of essence.

Work Support Management Reporting

This is a robust reporting package that will enable the call center to measure and record the performance of the WSM agents as well as the agents who require assistance.

One to Many

A WSM agent must be able to handle more than one Web chat at a time. For an internal application, this will be easily performed. Just like a supervisor who walks the floor and supports multiple agents, a WSM Web chatter can support multiple calls. This is the key to reducing costs. Today, we use Level Two personnel to support the front line by walking around, being available for a call, or taking the call over completely—all of which are inefficient.

Web Collaboration / Forms Sharing

Each of these features increases the likelihood that the WSM agent can support the agent and their problem. Any ability that we provide that allows a Level Two person to help the agent out by either working on the same forms or actually showing the rep where to go is positive. (Note: The ability to take over the agent's desktop would also be a feature that would benefit the process.)

Workstation Integration

This technology allows the host application to integrate with the Web messaging so the agent does not have to retype the problem or issue unless absolutely necessary. As the problem evolves, the application is able to transfer the important information directly into the instant messaging application. This is important because with high turnover and complicated transactions agents get in trouble more than once. The benefit of being connected throughout the transaction provides Level Two personnel with the ability to help throughout the call. This also enables the WSM agent to provide support in a timely fashion.

Benefits of Work Support Management

WSM offers several significant benefits. Here are just a few:

Reduction of Talk Time

WSM will provide critical information from real-time experts. It is not encumbered by walking around, single phone lines, or dedicated resources. Sometimes we focus too hard on finding agents the answers. Many times the answer may simply be a question that the agent did not know to ask. This is especially true for new hires and newly trained personnel. Giving an agent the next question to ask can improve learning and retention. The reduction in talk time for these areas alone can be substantial.

Reduction of Transfers

Many sophisticated call centers have had to go to Level Two alternatives or skills-based routing for questions or areas that exceed the general call population training. WSM can reduce the size of this group and move some of these transactions back to the general call population. BenchmarkPortal research of high-tech support centers shows that, on average, there is one Level Two "expert" per 15 to 20 front-line technicians. These experts typically field difficult questions, take escalated calls, plus constantly mentor, train, and coach individuals on their teams.

Increased Up-Selling

WSM can provide real-time sales support with both the right question and the right answer at the time it is needed. There is no necessity to put customers on hold or to transfer them.

Reduction in Training Costs

WSM can be the key link between training and agent learning. Having the ability to provide non-dedicated real-time support is critical to this area. Training performance can immediately be supported as well as validated. The answer can be the real "answer" rather than just additional training.

Connectivity

Finally, WSM enables you to take advantage of company expertise anywhere in the organization at any time. The Web enables us to bring real-time resources to bear right at the moment they are needed. This is mission critical today when we rely so heavily on so few resources to support and "bail out" the rest of the organization.

> WSM enables you to take advantage of company expertise anywhere in the organization at any time.

Industries start with two simple building blocks. The first block is that the application either saves a company real money or increases their profit. The second building block requires vendors bold enough to make it happen and customers visionary enough to participate in the new venture. We know about the first step. Now where are the vendors and visionary customers?

Work Support Management can provide an immediate return with a minimal investment. Killer applications are few and far between. This is one of them.

WRAP-UP

- Web chat is quickly establishing its presence in our industry. We must be prepared to take the steps necessary to be successful with it.

- Work Support Management is an amazing way to increase the quality of service you can provide through Web chat.

- Work Support Management has the potential to increase productivity and lower costs. Isn't that what all companies hope to achieve?

CHAPTER 28: SKILLS-BASED ROUTING

A Shift in Thinking

The idea was simple, brilliant, and totally against the purest form of what a call center is supposed to be. Skills-based routing was the right answer to a question most call centers never wanted to ask. Call centers were built around a very simple principle—we take anonymous callers and connect them to homogenous agents. They conduct their interactions and move on to the next caller.

This enabled companies to invest in Automatic Call Distributors (ACD) to take these calls, queue them, provide announcements, and deliver them to the next agent. ACD purists reluctantly added Direct Inward Dial (DID) features to systems to deal with the individual requirements of a small group or some rogue element of the pure call center. Any distraction toward calls directed at individuals or smaller groups was seen as heresy and frowned upon.

The introduction of skills-based routing changed the paradigm for ACDs. The routing of calls to experts based on their skill became the desired standard rather than an abnormality.

> It is obvious that the benefits of skills-based routing have become the strengths of many call centers.

Whether the solution is provided by a switching manufacturer or by a CTI/CRM company, the potential for the solution has greatly enhanced the quality of the services.

Keeping It in Perspective

Let's be audacious here. Despite all the hype and excitement, skills-based routing is the second most important type of routing needed today. The first kind is unskilled-based routing!

Unskilled-based routing recognizes the reality of a call center and goes directly to the heart of the solution and to the challenges that a call center executive deals with on a daily basis. Unskilled-based routing is the routing of calls/interactions to agents who need training, verification of training, or skills verification. This process must be tied to the performance monitoring system to fulfill its role in the improvement and performance of the call center.

> Despite all the hype and excitement, skills-based routing is the second most important type of routing needed today. The first kind is unskilled-based routing!

There are four factors that make this a necessity in a call center:

1. Call center turnover is running at over 30 percent per year, according to the latest Purdue University study. This means that in a 200-agent call center, almost one-third of the people (60) will be new employees each year. There is no consistency to the time and amount of turnover. Most call centers don't implement even one-third of their call centers with skills-based routing, yet 30 percent of their employees will be new every 12 months.

2. The training time necessary to bring an agent up to speed is increasing. This time is dependent on the degree of difficulty of the interactions the agents are performing. Simpler interaction call centers usually have much shorter training periods (sometimes as little as one or two weeks), while more complex interactions can take up to 10 or 12 weeks of training, with proficiency coming 4 to 6 weeks after that. Voice response continues to be the most prevalent technology within a call center. VRUs continue to take the "simpler" calls. This leaves more complicated calls that require more training.

3. Online training and "spot training" are becoming a reality with the addition of new requirements and new technology to serve those needs. This enables call centers to work on continuous improvement throughout the year. We are in a better position to do additional training and capabilities on an ongoing basis.

4. The universal agent is the present, not the future. Agents are given new requirements and tasks on a monthly basis. This is compounded by the new Web and e-mail interaction requirements. The job becomes more complicated each year. Call center representative is one the very few jobs in the world that continues to have increased responsibilities and not necessarily increased pay.

These four factors scream for unskilled-based routing. Here is hypothetical example of the need for unskilled-based routing:

A new agent has just been released from his or her initial training class. We put the new agent on the floor. We now purposely send calls to this agent using CTI. (All training experts will admit that repetition creates better proficiency and retention of what has been learned.) We implement our performance monitoring system to record this same interaction so we have a record of the call. We then review the call using our normal monitoring procedure.

This affords the company an understanding of what was taught, how well it was taught, and how well the agent performed. This same scenario would be used for verifying the skills of agents before they were given a skill level. This would allow us to be more accurate in the implementation of skills in the call center. Finally, we use this same procedure for any new training that we have in the center. We purposely send this new type of interaction to the newly trained agent, and we monitor that interaction. We can now verify the performance as well as the success of our training.

All of this information will be gathered in the quality monitoring database, which can then feed additional training, skill changes, and training curriculum.

> Unskilled-based routing takes advantage of the investments we have made in our call center.

It uses CTI, skills-based routing, recording, quality scoring, and training. The advantage of this type of integration can be seen at many levels. The benefits include decreased talk time, decreased hold times, increased sales conversions, and a reduction of transfers. The financial impact is also significant. Any changes that we can make to get an agent up to speed more quickly and with more quality will provide substantial financial benefits.

Unskilled-based routing focuses on solving the turnover challenge that every call center executive must face. Without a sustainable program of improvement in getting agents up to speed and keeping them current, we increase our risk of failure.

Unskilled-based routing takes direct aim at one of the biggest deterrents to quality and productivity. It gives us a solution to deal with the problem. It enables us to focus on the agents and help them to get better at their jobs sooner. We spend millions on training, and yet we have not mastered the ability to make sure we are delivering high quality service to all involved.

Skills-based routing is important; it is the SECOND most important type of routing we need in our call centers today.

WRAP-UP

- Skills-based routing has greatly enhanced the quality of service in many call centers. However, it must co-exist with unskilled-based routing.

- Unskilled-based routing is essential in many areas, including training and verifying the skills of agents.

Priorities

I recently had the opportunity to visit Burlington Northern Railroad headquarters just on the outskirts of Fort Worth. The headquarters also houses Burlington Northern's call center, operations center, and a beautiful museum. I, along with a group of other presidents from YPO (Young Presidents Organization), had been invited to a dinner in one of the railroad cars and was given a chance to view the company facilities.

Normally, we listen to a speaker for about 45 minutes, and then the group and their spouses have dinner. As the evening began, several Burlington Northern employees took us to an amphitheater-type classroom with about 150 theater seats. A huge curtain hung behind the speaker's table. We knew something was hidden behind the curtain, and we were going to get a chance to see it. We just didn't know what was it was.

Our welcoming speaker from Burlington Northern was in charge of security at the facility. He began his speech by thanking us for being there, quickly adding that the emergency exits were located on either side of the room. He said that he and his assistant would lead us out those doors in the case of an emergency. He further described what the alarms would sound like if that situation occurred. He added that the facility we were in was made of reinforced steel and cement and could withstand even the most powerful tornado.

My wife turned to me and asked, "Was this going to be some sort of a Disneyland ride?" I looked around the room, and everyone had a look of anticipation on their face, wondering what might happen next. The security expert then let us know that he was trained in first aid and CPR. He asked for an additional assistant from the audience who also knew CPR and waited patiently until someone raised their hand and agreed to help.

After finishing a short safety talk, he opened the curtains to show a spectacular view of the operations center. He told us a little bit about the center and then introduced the next speaker. There was no ride, no danger, not even a tiny scare. I was stunned at first. What was that all about? Security, alarms, CPR, tornados, and then not even the slightest sign of danger. Then it hit me, KAPOW!

This is what the security person saw when he entered a room of people. This was his priority, his area of expertise. He was asked to introduce the company to a group of executives, and we were able to see a glimpse of it through his eyes. He saw danger signs, emergencies, reinforced steel, and potential CPR assistants when he viewed a crowd.

Furthermore, that is what Burlington Northern's culture is built on. The company is in a very dangerous business, and this type of opening comment permeates all of their company meetings whether internal and external. Burlington Northern executives want safety to be their biggest focus.

Although there were several other speakers, none of them were executives from Burlington Northern. Looking back, there was nothing the company could have ever said to give us a feel for the business that would have been better than what the security person had done for us. His perspective gave us a perfect glimpse of Burlington Northern and its priorities.

What are your priorities? What would people see if they had a "perfect glimpse" of your priorities? Steven Covey's second habit of highly successful people is "Put first things first." In its simplest form, he asks us to take stock of our lives (note I said "lives," not "business priorities") and put the most important things first.

The key is to combine all areas of your life, year, month, week, and day into one large integrated time. Basically, we get to breathe. Now what's most important and how do we take advantage of that breath?

For me that makes my priority:

1. God
2. Wife
3. Kids
4. Health
5. Work.

That's right. Work is fifth on the list, and it should be for you, too. Let me be perfectly clear that I am not perfect by a very, very long shot, but I have learned through much tribulation what is important in my life. If your priorities are not what they should be, you can change today. My responsibility is to get in your face and ask you the questions.

Movie Quote:
"It's all about one thing!"
   —Jack Palance in *City Slickers* [8]

Overview: Billy Crystal takes off with his friends for a week of cattle herding. In the movie, Curly, a crusty old cowboy, is talking about life and its meaning. When Billy Crystal asks him what the "one thing" is, Curly responds that the "one thing" for everyone is different.

Personal Comment: For me, the one thing is my relationship with Jesus Christ. I fall way short in so many ways. It is only through my relationship with God that I even have a chance to do anything. It took me a long time to reconcile where I fit in the puzzle. I eventually figured out how small I really am and how large and amazing the grace of God is. It is by His sheer grace that we breathe, have our health, jobs, or anything else. The alternative for me is that everything and everyone are all random and truly have no meaning or purpose. There is a verse in the Bible, Hebrews 11:1, which says: "Faith is believing in what you hope for and being certain of what you do not see." I can see it in my changed life and the life of others. My hope is that you will find this same "one thing" out for yourself.

Each one of us in our own way was impacted by the tragedy in New York, Pennsylvania, and Washington on September 11, 2001. The image of devastated people walking the streets with pictures of their loved ones is still implanted in my mind. I don't think the people who were walking the streets were business associates, competitors, or former employees of the victims. They were the wives, husbands, kids, moms, and dads. They say that after a tremendous punch in the gut we all take a hard look at our priorities. Did this event make you look? Did you decide that it is time to make some changes?

> If your priorities are not what they should be, you can change today.

Don't miss the ballgame, church ministry, exercise time, school event, or time around the dinner table. It's not worth it. For example, in the past 11 years I have tried to coach as many of my kids' teams and attend as many events as I can. There are very few that I have missed. There is no reason to miss these events. I know you have all heard the line "Very few people say when they were older that they wished they had worked more in their life." When people are standing at your tombstone, especially your family, please don't have them thinking first, "He was a great businessman," or "She could really close a deal."

Two Important Rules of Life and Business

Here are two business rules that are very important whether you are running a business, answering calls, or working in a donut shop. Let's integrate them with both our business and our personal lives.

Rule 1

There are two questions that you must obtain a "yes" to in order to sell someone something: "Do they have a problem?" and "Do they care?" Without a positive response to both questions, it is virtually impossible to sell anything to anyone.

Someone once put the sales process to me in that very plain and simple statement. First, do they have a problem? One of the key sales components is to understand or establish a customer's pain. This is necessary to allow your product or service to reduce that pain. Notice that I said, "understand or establish." Many times, if not most times, a customer or client already knows what their pain is. You won't have to work in a call center long to see the pain of the customer. However, in rare instances, you have to establish the pain for the customer because he or she can't see it.

The second part of the equation is "Do they care?" A customer can have the largest problem in the world, but you still can't sell anything until they care enough to purchase. This could be impacted by a number of factors. One of the challenges of the call monitoring industry is the perception (wrongly I might add) that this technology is further down the "food chain" from the acquisition of other technology.

The client cares about quality but not as much as say screen pops. Another example is the person you are selling to may only be a recommender and not the final decision maker. In this instance, they may not care enough to get senior management involved or put the time and energy in to get through purchasing or contracts. Finally, despite all the right reasons and enough pain to open a hospital, some clients just don't see it or want to see the opportunity that is right in front of them.

> A customer can have the largest problem in the world,
> but you still can't sell anything until they care enough
> to purchase.

Do they have a problem and do they care? It affects us in our personal lives as well.

Six years ago I had the privilege of going to a seminar with a group of senior executives. We met in small groups and the seminar leader asked us a question. "What is the best thing and the worst thing that has happened to you in the last 90 days?" The first guy said he had just closed a huge deal with IBM. It was the largest deal he had ever made and it really was the pinnacle of his career. He also stated that his grandmother had passed away. Another guy said he had just received a promotion and really felt he was on his way to great success. He also had recently been sick. Another guy had recently achieved a financial windfall that had made him a multi-millionaire. He had also lost a grandparent.

When they got to me I told them that I had struggled with a pretty bad cold the previous month and that my nine-year-old daughter's soccer team, the Rockets, had beat the Cowgirls. After a stunned moment of silence, my counterparts lowered their raised eyebrows and asked me to explain. My daughter Christine played on a soccer team called the Rockets. The girls had been playing together since they were five years old. Each year they played a team called the Cowgirls, and every year they lost. They had been losing twice a year for four years

The Cowgirls were a machine, or at least as close to a machine as a nine-year-old girls' recreation team can be. They had the best talent, the best equipment, and two very on-purpose coaches who knew how to win. They had been practicing on the rest of us for five years. I was one of seven coaches on our team. The head coach had told the dads that anyone who wanted to coach could. There was only one or two of us that really knew soccer, but the rest of us were really enthusiastic and took our direction from the head coach and the other coach who knew something about the game.

It was quite a sight each week to see seven and sometimes eight dads running up and down the sidelines shouting encouragement and probably wrong advice to the girls.

We were playing the Cowgirls once again, and it was naturally our biggest game of the year. After the first half, the score was tied at 0–0. In the second half, my daughter, who normally played defense, got a breakaway and scored one of her only goals of the year. We held on to finish the game with a one-goal lead. At the end of the game, when the referee blew the whistle two times to signify time had expired, it was as if time stood still.

I saw the girls screaming for joy, I turned and saw the moms and dads in the stands crying and yelling, all the coaches were dancing and screaming with excitement, and my daughter had the proudest smile that dads dream about for their kids. That was the best 45 seconds that I had in the last 90 days.

There was no business meeting, no new client, no golf game that could ever have taken the place of that moment. Imagine if I had missed it. Do you have a problem in this area? Do you care? Are the Rockets playing the Cowgirls this weekend?

Rule 2

Backlog solves all problems.

A very smart person once told me that, and it is very true. Backlog is the amount of sales or business that you have already sold and is waiting to become revenue. The more that you have, the easier your job is in every area of the company. It helps us to plan our manufacturing, shipments, and installations, if necessary. It helps us understand how much revenue we can expect and how much profit or loss. Nothing warms the heart of both executives and agents more than backlog in a company. It is the very best form or security for everyone from the very top to the very bottom of the organization.

Backlog breeds confidence and a feeling of success. Companies thrive on confidence and build on success. In fact, success is contagious. It is inevitable that where there is success, more will follow. There are very few problems that cannot be surmounted in business when you have backlog.

> Nothing warms the heart of both executives and agents more than backlog in a company. It is the very best form of security for everyone from the very top to the very bottom of the organization.

Each one of us builds backlog every day in our lives. We pursue our work and our personal lives weekly, daily, and hourly. With each amount of time spent, we build a backlog of moments and memories that we carry with us for the remainder of our lives. Our ability to build this backlog helps us endure the more painful moments of our business and personal lives. It is not hard for me to be driven to my knees by the sheer weight of the recognition that it is by the grace of God that I have eyes to see, legs to walk, a capacity to think, and a heart to love. It is the things that we take for granted in our backlog that destroy us in a simple moment if they are lost.

Okay, Michael, what does this have to do with call centers and business? This is a pretty heavy way to finish a chapter. It is. I want to take you back to one of the very first things that we said when describing a call center. We called it the Four-Minute Market, and we said:

"This market is built on a premise that a company usually has less than 240 seconds to solve a problem or gain an opportunity, either over the phone, Web, or e-mail, using for the most part entry-level people and a 30 percent turnover rate. We have to create, delight, and retain customers in less time that it takes to boil an egg. We have to do it millions of times a year and with quality. In this industry, one extra second with a customer or a client from a large company is worth hundreds of thousands of dollars."

"Our industry accomplishes this task, for the most part, never meeting the customers, never knowing when they will arrive or when they will leave. We do this with very little fanfare, and for many years, we did it with little technology and few standards. This incredible industry is performing miracles in the business world and unfortunately most leaders and executives don't recognize the value they possess nor appreciate the contribution that their call centers make."

Each day our lives are filled with 240-second moments and opportunities to make a difference in this world. We can spend our time and efforts making a difference in someone else's backlog while filling our own backlog with the joy of service. We need look no further than the events of September 2001 in this country to see that our time is limited and, more importantly, we don't control when the clock runs out.

Why not treat our life as if it were a call in a call center? Why not create, retain, and delight friends, family, co-workers, and strangers? Why not do it millions of times each year? Why not recognize that even one second is precious and worth hundreds of thousands of dollars to each one of us?

> Why not treat our lives as if it were one call in a call center? Why not create, retain, and delight friends, family, co-workers, and strangers?

Why not make a difference to strangers no matter what their commitment to us? Why not make our relationships real, alive, and obnoxiously special each and every day? Why not perform miracles every day in the business world that fill your backlog and the backlog of those around you?

If you think about it, we who work in call centers have a precious perspective on just how fast life can move and how fleeting our contacts with other people are. If we want to make a difference, we need to be prepared, move quickly, and do it with quality. If we don't, we affect the lifetime value of our customers. What a great lesson for life!

If you have read this book, you know that I believe in God. He is the reason that we exist and the reason that we breathe. Each day the announcement of our lives should say: "Thank you for calling. Your **life** may be monitored or recorded for quality purposes..."

Please remember this statement when you wake up each morning, set your priorities, and go off to your call centers.

The clock is ticking... be audacious...get jazzed...make a difference.

WRAP-UP

- Priorities affect a person's whole outlook on life and business. Reevaluate yours to see if they are what they should be.

- People must recognize their problems and be willing to fix them before solutions can occur and sales can be made.

- Backlog brings comfort and security to both our businesses and our personal lives.

Statement by Michael Tamer

President of Teknekron Infoswitch

before the

Senate Subcommittee for Electronic Monitoring

and Privacy in the Workforce

June 22, 1993

Mr. Chairman and Members of the subcommittee, I appreciate the opportunity to speak before this Committee on legislation that may have a profound effect on my company, Teknekron Infoswitch Corporation, and the industry it serves, the call center marketplace.

Teknekron has been in the Call Center marketplace in excess of 15 years as a provider of telecommunications technology and services to Call Centers. Call Centers are integral parts of businesses that provide customer service to predominantly inbound callers over the telephone. Businesses utilize Call Centers either for revenue generation such as airline sales, insurance transactions, or catalogue sales; or for revenue protection such as banking transactions (credit management), public utility services or computer support activities. For these businesses, the ability to evaluate the effectiveness and competitiveness of their Call Center operations is absolutely critical with this ability being largely dependent upon obtaining reliable quantitative and qualitative data through electronic monitoring. We believe S.984, if not substantially revised, not only will harm businesses but ultimately, and most importantly, their employees and customers.

This is not to say that some portions of the legislation are not good, in fact some sections are very well done. Specifically Section 4 of the legislation, detailing the contents of notice to employees is by and large a needed element in the workplace. Nor, obviously, would we object to the legislation's privacy protections for locations such as bathrooms and locker rooms. This type of intrusive monitoring is patently offensive. But frankly, we believe that the definitions in the legislation are too broad and ambiguous, and that Sections 5,7,and 8 are largely unworkable. These sections construct artificial parameters without regard to the uniqueness of different industries and the complexities involved. While we may be submitting more specific legislative comments later to the Committee staff on these and other matters, let me address our chief concerns now:

1. This legislation impacts work products.

   In the Call Center environment, an agent's handling of a customer's call for placing an order, or inquiring about service, is that agent's work product.

2. A fundamental concept of business is the need to quantify and qualify an employees' work product.

   The ability to manage a business depends on the ability to review employees' work product (in the Call Center service business, this includes such areas as verification that proper etiquette was followed, appropriate pricing and product information was disclosed, and that an adequate number of transactions are processed).

3. Employees need to understand that their work product is serving the customer by telephone.

   Every employee, in whatever capacity, is subject to performance evaluation. In the Call Center environment, it is simply that this evaluation involves successfully processing telephone-related transactions.

4. This legislation will adversely affect industry initiatives focusing on Total Quality Management (TQM).

U.S. Companies have found it increasingly important to perform qualitative and quantitative evaluations in their efforts to compete in the global marketplace. While the legislation recognizes distinctions in continuous monitoring and random access monitoring, the restrictions contained in Sections 5, 6, and 8, along with the broadly based definitions, may ultimately preclude initiatives in TQM.

Monitoring inbound calls in a Call Center environment protects a company, its employees and its customers, as it allows for an accurate and effective evaluation of the quality and quantity of services provided by an employee to a company's customers. Quantitative measurements are not new (quantum measurements have frequently been an element of the workplace in job positions ranging from salespeople to assembly line workers). Nor, obviously, are qualitative measurements. What is new is the evolution of technology in making such measurements. We appreciate that an employee needs to be protected from excessively intrusive monitoring. We also believe employers need to be protected from over-zealous monitoring by supervisors, which ultimately contributes to a decline in morale and productivity. The legislation, as drafted, protects neither. We suggest there are alternative methods for providing this protection other than that proposed in the legislation (specifically the tenure caps, and notice windows). These methods are developed by harnessing available technology to assure fair and objective treatment of employees, while providing immensely improved data and information collection to employers.

Technology currently exists and is used by our customers to establish a process which enhances the work product and protects the employee, the employer, and the customer. For instance, to assure accuracy and consistency in monitoring, parameters and constraints may be automatically established (by length of call, by time of day, by type of product); for more efficient evaluation, a supervisor may prerecord a session and review it at a more convenient time with opportunity for playback; for use as an employee training tool, a supervisor's notes and comments may be input to be considered later by the employee; for accuracy in performance evaluations, an employee may pre-select and experiment with self-selected parameters; and perhaps most importantly, the monitor may be monitored. This means that any evaluation system used for an employee may also include a similar system for the monitor (the supervisor). The monitor's actual scoring trends can be reviewed in relationship to their peers and the company's standards, and the monitoring can also include the ability to decipher and discriminatory practices of the reviewing supervisor such as between the sexes, the aging, the disabled or minorities. This can ensure not only fair recording of the data but strong confidence by the employee that the people monitoring cannot abuse their employees.

The telephone center for inbound calling is a rising area of employment in this country. There are estimated to be over 40,000 call centers in existence today. Companies are increasingly recognizing that customers can be served over the phone with high quality of service and at a reduced cost compared to face-to-face communication. New job market opportunities such as telecommuting, which is the performance of the telephone service representative functions at home, have opened up tremendous opportunities for the disabled, the elderly and the working parent. Telecommuting jobs are expected to increase dramatically for the rest of this decade. Equally benefited are those who, for one reason or another, cannot physically go to a place of business, and yet can receive virtually any service over the phone. The legislation, if not significantly modified, will adversely affect these job markets.

In conclusion, Teknekron Infoswitch believes that when used fairly and ethically, monitoring in the Call Center environment can benefit the employer, the employee, and the customer. As mentioned before, we believe that this protection cannot be ensured by artificial constraints, but instead by an equitable process. In this regard, Teknekron Infoswitch has the following recommendations for any electronic monitoring legislation that this Committee and the Senate may consider:

1. First and most importantly, the monitors must be monitored.

2. Monitoring may only be used for business purposes.

3. Data and information in whatever form (visual, audio, etc.) must be recorded, stored, and made available for the protection of the employee and the employer for a reasonable period of time.

4. All similarly situated employees must be monitored consistently (in other words, one group may not be monitored only in the morning when they are well rested and another only late in the day).

5. Disclosure must be made to employees of the substance of the monitoring (in other words, what quantitative and qualitative factors are being evaluated and how are those factors interrelated).

6. Monitoring must be disclosed (but restraints, especially time restraints, if any, must be created with enough flexibility to avoid destroying the accuracy and reliability of the information collected).

Finally, Mr. Chairman and Members of the Subcommittee, I believe it would be enormously beneficial to this Committee if the technology currently utilized by our customers could be demonstrated. This could provide Senators and their staffs with an understanding of how technology protects workers from abuse while providing businesses with information vital to their competitiveness and successful service to their customers. Mr. Chairman, I cannot overemphasize how proud you would be of the impressive service America's leading companies provide to the ultimate and most important customer, the American people.

Thank you for the opportunity to provide you with information on this very important subject. We look forward to working with the Committee on this matter.

REFERENCES

1. *Jaws*. Dir. Stephen Spielberg, Universal Studios, 1975.

2. *Teenage Mutant Ninja Turtles*. Dir. Steve Barron, New Line Cinema, 1990.

3. *The Sandlot*. Dir. David M. Evans, Twentieth Century Fox, 1993.

4. *A Few Good Men*. Dir. Rob Reiner, Columbia Pictures, 1992.

5. *Top Gun*. Dir. Tony Scott, Paramount Pictures, 1986.

6. *The Natural*. Dir. Barry Levinson, Columbia Tristar, 1984.

7. *The Terminator*. Dir. James Cameron, 1984.

8. *City Slickers*. Dir. Ron Underwood, Castle Rock Entertainment 1991.

A

ADP Corporation 156
American Airlines 19
American Express
    Corporation 13
Aspect
    Telecommunications 11
AT&T Wireless 155

B

Bana Box 105
bell curve 65
BenchmarkPortal ... 23, 81, 118
Blue Cross/Blue Shield of
    Alabama 39, 44, 153
Budget Rent a Car 157
Burlington Northern's 189

C

Cigna Corporation 154
Computer Telephone
    Integration 22
Continental Airlines 11
Convergys Corporation 156

D

Datamonitor 101
Datapoint Corporation 11
Dataquest 11
definition 5
Delta Airlines 111
Direct Inward Dial (DID) 20
Dr. Dick Grote 48

E

Empowerment 86

F

Ford Motor Company
    Business Assistance
    Center 153
Four Seasons Hotel 171

G

GE Answer Center 12
General Electric 154
Georgia Power
    Corporation 156
goals 18, 38, 44, 67, 68, 72,
    78, 79, 80, 82, 96, 97,
    105, 111, 112, 118, 122,
    131, 132, 156, 194

H

Hierarchy of Needs 35, 36,
    37, 40

I

IBM 44, 154
incentive programs 45
Incoming Calls
    Management Institute 11
Infoswitch ACD 12
integration 169, 187

J

Jazzed People 39
jet 85, 98

K

Kaiser Permanente 156

M

Maslow 36
monitoring ..... xi, 13, 38, 60, 63,
    84, 108, 117, 118, 121,
    125, 126, 127, 128, 129,
    130, 131, 133, 134, 135,
    136, 147, 148, 149, 150,
    151, 168, 169, 181, 186,
    187, 192, 199, 200, 201,
    202
Movie Quote 24, 44, 73, 84,
    86, 99, 106, 191

N

Nintendo 101
Nordstrom's 104
Nuance Communications 19

P

Palm 173
Predictive Dialer 13
profitability 6, 79, 80, 180
Purdue University .. 26, 81, 186

R

rewards 4, 39, 40, 52, 56,
    57, 58, 108, 136, 170
Rewards 56
Ritz Carlton Hotel 103
Rockwell International 12

S

Seagull Management 89
Skills-based routing 21
Southwest Airlines 79
Starbucks 104

Steven Covey 190
Subcommittee for
    Electronic Monitoring
    and Privacy 147

T

Talbots 101
Teknekron Infoswitch
    Corporation 13
Temporary Jobs 85
training ... 13, 18, 22, 25, 26, 41,
    48, 68, 83, 113, 119,
    121, 122, 128, 141, 150,
    180, 181, 183, 185, 186,
    187, 188, 201
turnover 3, 22, 32, 41, 53, 62,
    95, 96, 121, 182, 186,
    187, 195

U

U.S. Surgical Corporation 13
universal agent 22

V

Verizon 77

W

Witness Systems 13
WRAP-UP 9, 15, 27, 32,
    40, 46, 49, 54, 58, 63,
    68, 80, 88, 93, 100, 108,
    116, 123, 130, 137, 145,
    151, 157, 166, 170, 177,
    184, 188, 197

Y

Young Presidents
    Organization 189

Michael J. Tamer, former President and CEO of Teknekron Infoswitch and e-talk Corporation, has pioneered the delivery and measurement of quality in the Customer Contact industry. An 18-year industry veteran, Tamer has been teaching the benefits of quality to organizations all over the world, including the United States Senate. He is an expert in Customer Relationship Management, helping organizations find new ways to sell and service their customers.

As a featured speaker for industry seminars and conferences, Tamer's innovative approach to audience participation, which involves multi-media and real life experiences, brings a refreshing and exciting change to the world of Call Center Customer Service. He has a Bachelor of Science degree from the University of Rhode Island and resides with his family in the Dallas-Fort Worth metroplex.

Also Available From BenchmarkPortal, Inc.

e-Business Customer Service
By Jon Anton and Michael Hoeck
With the advent of e-business technology, we suddenly find ourselves with completely different customer service channels. The old paradigms are gone forever. This books details how to measure and manage e-business customer service. The book describes the key performance indicators for these new channels, and it describes how to manage by these new rules of engagement with specific metrics. Managing customer service in this "new age" is different, it is challenging, and it is impossible to migrate from the old to the new without reading this book.
ISBN 0-9630464-9-7

Forward Business Intelligence
By Jon Anton and Natalie Petouhoff
"Case Studies of Customer Analytics" In this book we describe sixteen case studies of how to process caller data into actionable reports for real-time management decision-making. Reporting examples include, ad hoc reports, exception reports, threshold reports, drill-down reports, and statistical reports.
ISBN 0-9630464-4-6

How to Conduct a Call Center Performance Audit: A to Z
By Jon Anton and Dru Phelps
Call centers are an important company asset, but also a very expensive one. By learning to conduct a performance audit, readers will be able to understand over fifty specific aspects of a call center that must be running smoothly in order to achieve maximum performance in both efficiency and effectiveness of handling inbound customer calls.
ISBN 0-9630464-6-2

Integrating People with Processes and CRM Technology
By Jon Anton, Natalie Petouhoff, & Lisa Schwartz
This book contains valuable information regarding the "people" side of technology initiatives. Many companies buy the best hardware and software, and spend thousands of dollars implementing technology only to find out that the employees resist the changes, and do not fully adopt the new, and possibly, improved processes. By understanding how to manage people during change, managers will see a much quicker ROI on their technology initiatives.
ISBN 0-9630464-3-8

Also Available From BenchmarkPortal, Inc.

Minimizing Agent Turnover

By Jon Anton and Anita Rockwell

Some agent turnover can be functional, but most turnover is dysfunctional and can be very expensive. This book explores the types of turnover, including internal versus external; and documents the typical causes of agent turnover. Most importantly, this book describes a methodology for diagnosing the root causes of your agent turnover, and suggests improvement initiatives to minimize agent turnover at your customer contact center.

ISBN 0-9630464-2-X

Selecting a Teleservices Partner

By Jon Anton and Lori Carr

This book tackles one of today's hottest topics: Customer Contact Outsourcing. Companies are in a quandary about the myriad of teleservices questions they're faced with, such as deciding to outsource, cost / benefit analysis, RFP development, proposal assessment, vendor selection, contractual requirements, service level performance measurement, and managing an ongoing teleservices relationship. With the authors help, readers will find this complex issue straightforward to approach, understand, and implement.

ISBN 0-9630464-8-9

The Four-Minute Customer

By Michael Tamer

This is a very unique book directed at developing and maintaining "Top Reps" that are uniquely motivated to deliver the highest possible quality of caller customer service at your center. Learn what it takes to find and lead the best of the best. Don't settle for mediocrity. Instead, learn how to manage the best in class customer contact center by attracting and keeping Top Reps at your organization.

ISBN 0-9630464-1-1

The Technology of CRM

By Jon Anton, Bob Vilsoet, and Natalie L. Petouhoff

From our research on the American consumer, it has become very clear that potentially the best customer service strategy is "to offer every possible channel for the customer to help themselves, i.e., self-service." Customer actuated service is mostly driven by technology, and the "art" of self-service is to ensure that the technology is intuitive, easy to use, and that the customer is rewarded for "having done the job themselves." This book delves into all the technology solutions that enable self-service. The reader will find a robust description of the technology alternatives, and many examples of how self-service is saving companies money, while at the same time satisfying customers.

ISBN 0-9630464-7-0

Order Form

Billing Information: **Shipping Information** (if different):

Name	
Company	
Address	
Address 2	
City/St/Zip	
Phone	

Please charge my: _____Visa   _____Mastercard

Card Number

Expiration Date

Signature

I've enclosed a check in the amount of

Purchase Order Number

Book Title	Amt*	Qty	Total
Benchmarking For Profits!	$11.95		
Call Center Management	$46.95		
Call Center Simulation	$48.95		
e-Business Customer Service	$44.00		
Forward Business Intelligence	$29.99		
How to Conduct a Call Center Performance Audit: A to Z	$34.49		
Integrating People with Processes and CRM Technology	$39.99		
Listening to the Voice of the Customer	$33.95		
Minimizing Agent Turnover	$39.99		
Selecting a Teleservices Partner	$34.99		
The Four-Minute Customer	$34.99		
The Technology of CRM	$39.99		
Books Total			
Shipping and Handling *For all U.S. addresses, $5.00 for the first book, $3.00 for each additional book.* *For all International addresses, books must be* **pre-paid** *and must include a shipping and handling charge of $25.00 for the first book and $10 for each additional book.*			
Total Amount Due**			

*Call for volume and pre-order discounts available (805-614-0123 Ext. 10)
**State sales tax will be added where applicable

For other books, tapes, and videos visit our online store:

http://www.benchmarkportal.com/store/index.taf

Send all orders to:

BenchmarkPortal, Inc.

3130 Skyway Drive, Suite 702

Santa Maria, CA 93455-1817

For quick service, fax your order to: (805) 614-0055

For questions about your order, please call: (805) 614-0123 Ext. 10